DISCOVER TO RECOVER

DISCOVER TO RECOVER

Overcome adversity, live in prosperity and fulfil your destiny

Emmanuel C. Mbakwe

WORD2PRINT

A Division of One-Touch UK

DISCOVER TO RECOVER

Unless otherwise stated, all Scripture quotations are taken from The
New International Version (NIV) of the Bible. Scriptures taken from
Holy Bible, New International Version®, NIV® Copyright © 1973, 1978,
1984, 2011 by Biblica, Inc.® Used by permission. All rights reserved
worldwide.
First published in the United Kingdom in 2013 by Word2Print

www.word2print.com

ISBN 978-1-908588-05-0

A CIP catalogue record for this title is available from the British Library

Printed by
CPI Group UK CR0 4YY

Dedication

This book is dedicated to my dearest wife Helen, and my daughters - Christiana Amarachi, Deborah Kelechi, Joy Odochi and Priscilla Akachi. Thank you for your constant love, support, and appreciation. I love you all.

Table of Contents

Foreword

The pastoral task is one of the most precious and powerful vocations in which people are privileged to become involved. It often means celebrating the joys of birth and baptism, walking with individuals through new terms of experiences and successes. It allows us the vantage point from which to highlight the numerous good things which are quietly taking place in the midst of the madness of our world. But invariably it means taking up the rod and staff and gently guiding the flock through the thickets of our world's cultures dilemma.

Discover to Recover could be seen as a pastor with staff in hand. In this work, Emmanuel Mbakwe offers his own broad insights into the catalogue of social problems and crises facing our societies in general and life in Britain in particular. This book is a treatise on the life of Isaac in which Emmanuel elevates a brief but powerful incident in the patriarch's life to speak to us as a case study in trusting God during our crisis.

There is no pretense here that 'prosperity is a quick fix which comes by conjuring up God as a magician who gets me what I want regardless.' Rather, we are guided through some old foundational ideas and challenged to face down our crises through trust and obedience to God. Pastor Mbakwe is open to new ways of seeing the world but he is equally committed to the task of 'digging the old wells' which have been left to us by those who have preceded us in the journey.

If you're going through a famine, the important message of this book is that you can get to where you're going by digging the wells where you are. *Discover to Recover* is guidance from the heart of a pastor to those of us who want to do more than merely survive during a spiritual famine.

Rev Joel Edwards
Director
MICAH CHALLENGE INTERNATIONAL

Endorsement

You will surely find *Discover to Recover* to be a treasure-trove of timeless, godly wisdom. This book is a gift to *ordinary* people who want to live *extraordinary* lives for God. In these pages, Emmanuel Mbakwe mines the age old lessons embedded in the life of Isaac and lays out for us transformational, present-day insights. We may be tempted to overlook the apparently bland life of Isaac in comparison to the other biblical patriarchs like Abraham, Jacob and Joseph. Yet you will discover this book to be full of rich encouragement, practical challenges and Spirit-borne guidance. *Discover to Recover* will also give renewed hope to those who have experienced crisis, disappointment and hurt in their walk with Christ.

The story of Isaac is one of a simple man trying to live by faith while enduring much pressure and crisis. You will be coached through the process of allowing these to *make* you rather than *break* you. Emmanuel also does a colourful job of drawing on examples in business, economics, culture, politics, agriculture and world events to illustrate these principles. Get ready to have your sights lifted, your perspective clarified and your faith strengthened as you unfold this compelling blueprint for fulfilling your personal destiny in God!

R. Sonny Misar
Apostolic Pastor, Living Light Church, Winona, Minnesota, USA
Author of 'Journey to Authenticity'

Many desire to be successful and work towards it but only few people achieve it. If you really want to move from just desiring, planning and working hard to the place of actual achievement, then this book is a must read. Life is so short that by the time you gather enough wisdom and experience to live wisely, you are old and have no strength to do so. Great achievers learn from the lives of others and that is what Pastor Mbakwe sets forth so beautifully and powerfully in these pages.

Rev Dr Aaron Ami-Narh
Apostolic Church, Ghana

Acknowledgements

Discover to Recover is the crystallization of a long process that extends over more than five decades. As such I am grateful to God for all the people – my late parents, spiritual mentors, pastors and teachers – whose godly influence has undoubtedly left an imprint on my life. As have friends, former and current colleagues who have also been tools in the hands of God in shaping my thinking and character.

Many people have come to me over the years with words of encouragement; some have challenged me, while others have asked me when I would put my thoughts into print. Angela Sampah was the first person to speak to me boldly and directly. Thank you for your offer 21 years ago to type my manuscript whenever I was ready to write. This book is the first fruits of your words which have remained a constant prophetic challenge to me.

In life, we are able to rise to challenges, seize opportunities and achieve major goals because of the love and support of the people who see and believe in the gifts of God in us. Such is the case with the members and partners of Life Transformer Ministry (LTM). Some of you are more frontline than others, yet all of you are valued and cherished equally. Tope Aiyere, thank you for your energy and drive. May the joy of the Lord continue to be your strength. David Ogbonna, thank you for your encouragement and constancy in prayer. May the fire continue to burn brightly in your heart. Soji and Bose Oguntonade, thank you for the gift of your apartment in Spain to enable me write, away from distractions. May you be enriched in every good work. To Helen Moore and Fatima Ellams, thank you for your belief and commitment to the vision.

While I take responsibility for the final product I want to appreciate all those who have contributed in making this book a reality. A big thank you to Dr Muyiwa Olumoroti of Word2Print, whose significant input, wise counsel, support and challenge has helped to shape what you have in your hand. I thank Carl Appleby, whose generosity of spirit, professional editorial skills, and encouragement helped to significantly raise the bar of the final output. God bless you richly. Marcus Abbot, thank you for brokering the link with Carl. To Michael Babatunde, your creativity and profession-alism in designing the book cover is greatly appreciated.

Rev Joel Edwards - thank you for your generosity of spirit in agreeing to write the foreword. Also, thanks to Sonny Misar and Aaron Ami-Narh for agreeing to endorse *Discover to Recover*. I am sure there are many others worthy of acknowledgement. Please forgive me if you do not receive a specific mention. Your blessing is assured.

I want to end by expressing my gratitude to the Lord Jesus, whose grace and favour has made this book possible. Thank you, Lord!

Emmanuel C. Mbakwe
London, July 2013

Introduction

It does not matter who you are or where you come from, your skin colour, political or religious persuasion; your occupation, lineage, age, status, role or responsibility in life; each of us will experience times and seasons of crises and difficulties, when we need to discover answers for our breakout or breakthrough. This is true for individuals, particularly those with responsibility for leading others, such as parents, guardians, managers, directors, pastors and all whose influence are brought to bear on the lives of others on a daily basis. The same is true for families, communities, corporations, and, indeed, nations. Everyone needs to discover or rediscover in order to recover. Without discovery there can be no recovery.

There are no new truths under the sun; only old ones rediscovered. God has set in place eternal principles, which, if followed, will bring the follower to a place of prosperity and blessing. However, the problem is that we have a tendency to ignore the so-called elephant in the room, and lean towards the easy or comfortable, rather than focusing on the key issues.

Our natural tendency is to ignore God, avoid, and look away from, or fail to learn key lessons from the past. As humans, we would rather follow our own inclinations, search for novel and seemingly exciting four-wheel-drive solutions with the go-faster stripes, while the true answers are staring us right in the face. The result: we repeat the mistakes of history. When that happens, we blame others or look for other excuses. We run away at the first sign of trouble instead of standing our ground, working hard, and pushing through the tough times and testing moments.

The answers to all our problems and the keys to our recovery are close to hand. They are to be found in the word of God. To anyone who desires to make progress, rise higher, live prosperously and fulfil their God-given purpose on earth, God has something practical to say through the narrative of Isaac's life. The son of Abraham and the father of Jacob, Isaac has been said to be 'the ordinary son of an extraordinary father, and the ordinary father of an extraordinary son'. Isaac it seems was just 'ordinary'. Or was he? At first glance his life seems to be no more than a parenthesis between two exceptionally high achievers. Genesis 26 is the only chapter in the Bible that deals exclusively with Isaac. This seemingly quiet, unassuming, understated patriarch is placed centre stage by God. As we read carefully through the narrative, we see that his life has so much to teach us just like that of his father, Abraham.

This is a book about the recovery, progress, and fulfilment that comes from God and God alone; the sort that can only flow from God's generous revelation. It is recovery, progress and fulfilment that go beyond the material. Isaac found himself in the middle of some extraordinarily testing circumstances. During a famine, God told him to stay put and stay away from Egypt. He did. We explore the life-changing lessons that we can learn from his walk of obedience. We will also draw lessons from characters such as Moses, Abraham and others from the Bible, as well as people from our contemporary world.

If I were to summarise in a few words the central thesis of this book and the journey we are about to go on together, I would call it 'How to thrive in the midst of the downturns of life.' However, it goes beyond that. I invite you to come on this journey with me. As you read, carefully consider and follow the God-given and time-tested principles that were worked out in Isaac's life and that of others, and you too will experience the very best of the spiritual, material, physical and emotional blessings that God has for you.

Emmanuel C. Mbakwe
London, July 2013

Chapter 1

PROBLEMS, PRESSURES, AND CRISES

Now there was a famine in the land—besides the previous famine in Abraham's time—and Isaac went to Abimelek king of the Philistines in Gerar. (Genesis 26:1)

LIFE is marked by problems, pressures, and crises. These can be a crisis of health or wealth; of confidence or conflict. Whatever walk of life we come from, problems will always arise. No facet of life is problem-free. Life as we know it is full of issues and challenges for individuals, families, communities, cities and nations. Everywhere you turn, you will hear of physical, economic, social, emotional, psychological or spiritual problems, with people desperately crying out for a solution. The issues are major as well as minor. Even the so-called small problems multiply in number by the day and can become a tidal wave. It is however in these difficult times that we learn, grow and mature.

Society and life as we know it is on edge; a moral and

spiritual abyss looms large. Even the most optimistic among us acknowledge that we' face huge problems or a catalogue of crises in our world. There is definitely a crisis in the land. The clergy are generally no longer viewed as figures of moral authority in their communities. Theologians do not speak for and to the nation. Church leaders no longer play their God-ordained prophetic role in today's world. Communities are not only in a continual state of flux, but massively diverse in their beliefs, values, and social identities. The free movement of labour and capital across national frontiers reinforces this tendency towards diversity and diffusion. These have huge implications for the Church with regards to its mission. The impact of this on the Church, among others, is apostasy within, and ignorance and hostility in society, the consequent waning of moral authority and influence, with attendant damage to family life and community cohesion.

The month of August 2011 will be long remembered as one of the worst periods in peace time in many cities across the United Kingdom. Initially triggered in Tottenham, north London, on Saturday 6th August 2011, by the shooting of a young man by a policeman; what unfolded over two further nights, especially in London, Manchester and Birmingham, were scenes never before witnessed in the nation, not even in the Brixton riots of 1981, that of the Broadwater Farm estate in Tottenham, north London in 1985 or any of the other examples of civil disturbance in the past. What we saw, particularly in the first two nights, was a seemingly powerless police force, overwhelmed and swept aside by a tidal wave of violence, unbridled greed, wanton destruction of property and the brazen ransacking of stores, many of which were long established family businesses that provided employment to local people.

Shops were looted and burned down, as violence engulfed and destroyed already fragile relations in a number of the most vulnerable communities. Lives were lost; a horrific example being the three young men in Birmingham who were mowed down by a recklessly driven car. One major characteristic of what took place during the riots was that the damage was so widespread and the nature of the disturbance, the preponderance of young people and the fact that it cut across race and ethnic lines.

Fiery arguments, polemics, explanations and denunciations raged in the aftermath of what was one the most terrifying spates of violence, looting, and unrestrained carnage to have ever hit the city streets of Great Britain. Right across the political spectrum, amongst community leaders, historians, commentators, and religious leaders, local and national leaders of every persuasion weighed in with their views as to the reasons for the riots. Matters were not helped by inflammatory utterances by some notable figures.

The Prime Minister, David Cameron and former Premier, Tony Blair, clashed in their views as to the causes of the riots. Mr Cameron's belief was that the riots were symptomatic of moral decline in Britain. These were his exact words in the *Sunday Express* of 21st August 2011: 'The greed and thuggery we saw during the riots did not come out of nowhere. There are deep problems in our society that have been growing for a long time: a decline in responsibility, a rise in selfishness, a growing sense that individual rights come before anything else'. Mr Blair on his part dismissed that notion as 'highfalutin wail' which missed the point and ignored the real cause of the problem. In his view, there was no problem with moral standards in society generally. What we have, he says, is the existence of a minority of disaffected youth who are outside the mainstream of life in Britain. In an article in the *Observer* (Sunday 21st August 2011), he said, 'Britain, as a whole, is not in the grip of some general 'moral decline'. He went on to say that young people now were generally more respectable, more responsible and more hard-working than they were when he was young.

Similarly opposed views were expressed across the nation – in newsprint, on radio, television, social media outlets, blog sites, barber shops and other community meeting places. The arguments raged on for weeks and months, resurfacing frequently during court trials of the rioters. What is self-evident is that the consequences of the recent riots are far-reaching (I speak as an eye-witness to the Brixton riots of 1981). The wounds in communities across the cities that were affected are deep. Issues of poor educational attainment, lack of job opportunities, unemployment, debt, vulnerability, disaffection, marginalisation, family breakdowns and poverty present a perplexing amalgam of complex causes and symptoms in many communities. What is also clear is the strong divergence of views as to the underlying causes.

Judging from the differing perspectives offered by Prime Minster Cameron and former Premier Mr Blair, it is evident that we are a long way from a shared view of underlying causes. What is however clear, including among young people, is that there is a huge problem.

Most people agree that we have a major crisis in our cities.

Many speak of 'Broken Britain'. That view is not an exaggeration. Brokenness pervades many areas of national life, both in the moral and spiritual sphere. In my view, what happened during those dark days and nights in August 2011 is nothing other than a reflection of abject failure, deep rooted let-down on the part of all the key institutions whose role is to help build peaceful, strong, safe and successful communities, people, and nation. First, the family has failed. Second, government and politicians have failed. Educators and schools have failed. The police have failed. The Church, of which I am part, has also failed in many respects. Collectively, we have failed morally and spiritually. We have failed practically. We have failed to provide much-needed leadership.

The purpose here is not to apportion blame, but rather to first acknowledge the present condition and the root causes. A friend of mine uses an expression that resonates and comes back to me time and again. In seeking to address issues or problems, he uses the phrase 'the truth about today'. By that he means that there needs to be a shared view and acceptance of present realities. If we are to find solutions that go beyond the superficial, we must first agree there is a problem, identify root causes, before considering solution options.

What about the wider family life? What we are seeing today, particularly in the West, is that there is a ferocious assault on family life. The moral fabric of society is being shredded to pieces. The problem comes from a variety of sources and manifests itself in many ways. The traditional family is under tremendous attack by the forces of secularism. This is not a lament but recognition of where the tide is coming from. In the UK it is led, aided and abetted by a combination of forces, namely, those who conceive, shape and make policies, both inside and outside government: the media, interest groups and the main political parties, to name a few.

Traditional family set ups are breaking down, not just in the West, but around the world. Children are turning against their parents; families and relatives are in conflict. Children are being abandoned in droves by parents who either do not care, or are incapable, for one reason or another, to raise them. Children as young as 12 years of age are being treated for drink problems. A woman lay dead in her bed for four months in Southwark, London, before local council staff who came to collect her rent found her.

Marital and domestic violence is up. A report in the Guardian newspaper dated 7th March 2013 states: *The war against domestic violence was meant to have been won, with a 40% decline in incidents since 1995, according to the British Crime Survey. But, in worrying new figures, the charity Citizens Advice has reported a substantial increase in the number of people telling advisers they are victims.* There were 3,300 reported incidents between October and December 2012, an increase of 11% over the same period in the previous year. According to Home Office figures, 1.2 million women experienced domestic abuse last year in the UK, including half a million victims of sexual assault.

One of Amnesty International's advertisements in a national Daily portrays a very grim situation in communist China: "Li Yan's husband started beating her shortly after they got married. He stubbed cigarettes in her face, cut off one of her fingers and locked her out, near naked, on the balcony of their flat for hours in freezing weather." Despite asking for help from the authorities, there was no reprieve. She eventually had enough. In November of 2010, Yan allegedly beat her husband to death with a gun. For this Yan was sentenced to death by the Chinese authorities, hence the appeal by Amnesty International for Yan's life to be spared, given the extraordinary circumstances.

Additionally, we have gone from a world not so long ago where people were not getting enough food to eat to one today where over-eating and unhealthy eating habits are leading to a morbid obesity epidemic, attendant stress on the health services, and ultimately death of those individuals. Aircraft seats and other public service facilities, such as ambulances, are being re-designed to take account of a growing population of obese people. Smoking and alcohol abuse have become the cause of a majority of deaths in the world today, overtaking malnutrition and hunger as the main cause of premature death worldwide.

The current global economic meltdown has had a devastating effect all round. A study in the United Kingdom showed that two thirds of parents with one child said they could not afford to have a second because they were too poor. Ironically, in the poorest regions of the world, people who are barely able to afford the basic necessities of life continue to have children, often leaving those children to fend for themselves, or be driven into poorly paid labour, modern-day slavery, prostitution and all forms of abuse. Children are going to school hungry because they cannot afford to eat. I must hasten to add - that is not happening only in the remotest parts of Africa or Asia, but in Britain and in the USA. The growth of food banks across many towns and cities in the UK bears testimony to this. The UK *Guardian* newspaper on 5th March 2013, reported figures collected by the Trussell Trust which operates food bank networks, in which they announced that it will feed 280,000 people in 2012-13, up from 129,000 in 2011-12. It is now feared that this trend may continue into the year 2017 or beyond!

Over a million young people between the ages of 16-24 years are currently unemployed. The lofty hopes of a good job after university education for many have vanished into thin air. High calibre graduates with first or second class honours degrees are being offered menial jobs – in one case, an architectural design graduate had to settle for a job where he cleaned horse stables. At the end of 2012, unemployment in the Eurozone had reached an average of 12 per cent. In Greece alone, close to two-thirds of young people have nothing to do by way of formal employment. Many now have to choose between eating their food and heating their homes. One minute you read in the newspapers that a certain country or the world economy has beaten the recession; the next we hear is that they are heading for a double or even triple-dip recession.

There are significant trends that threaten to denude or even pauperise the next generation. There is evidence to show the escalating level of personal debt among students and young people. They take on huge loans to go to university, and yet when they come out there are no jobs. They then end up in a vicious cycle of debt and rising cost of living. Yet another key indicator of the depth of the financial malaise we are in is the exponential growth in UK High Streets of the so-called Payday Loan providers. These are the legalised loan sharks who prey on hard-pressed individuals. They advance generally low sums in loan at extraordinarily high interest rates – some of which are so high that the borrowers - often low income workers – are sunk further into debt as a result. These Payday Loan companies are so notorious that the UK government is now seeking to curb their activities.

In an effort to find a once-for-all solution or even dull the pain of personal crisis, many people engage in activities which only make matters worse. They borrow more and gamble. In the UK, over half a billion pounds (£650 million) was paid in penalty fees on credit card and bank accounts in 2011 by over 2 million people caught in late payment traps. According to a report by the London's *Evening Standard*, Britons who were hunting a fortune have gambled a total of 3.5 billion pounds on the National Lottery in the six months leading to October 2012. Only about half of that (1.9 billion) was paid out as prize money. The irony of this is that only a handful of people end up with a win, thereby leaving several millions to lick their wounds, or to continue to fund waste money, and for some, to plunge further into debt, all in a vain hope of hitting the jackpot.

Again according to the UK Office for National Statistics, the combined debt of households in the UK at the end of January 2013 was approximately £90 billion. In a population made up of 26 million households and families, this debt is equal to an average of £3,500 per household. Put simply, every home in the land owes!

There has been no let-up in this human misery brought

about by the economic pain. At the beginning of January 2012, the number of people being forced out of their homes by bailiffs rose by a fifth; and half of these were carried out by mortgage lenders. Unemployment continues to bite in all regions. Over 600,000 jobs have been lost in the UK public sector since the coalition government came to power in the summer of 2010. As the recessionary gloom deepens, the bankers, the so called masters of the universe, who by popular consensus brought the world to its knees, have not been immune. In London in September 2012, a 29-year-old city banker calmly took a sip of wine from her glass while dining in an upmarket restaurant, placed her hand bag on the floor, and leapt to her death from the rooftop of the diner. That sadly was the third death in a similar fashion from the same dining establishment. In another incident, a 48-year-old stockbroker in Daegu, South Korea, also jumped to his death from a high-rise apartment block after suffering heavy losses in the global market meltdown.

Stories abound of the astonishing and desperate things that people are prepared to do in order to survive. Moral values are discounted, ethics mean nothing, and long held standards are jettisoned in the mad scramble for survival. Hard pressed parents in some regions of the world are sending their children to sell their bodies to the highest bidder. Sexual exploitation and human trafficking have assumed global significance. Hardly a day passes without news of parents in certain parts of the world trying to sell their children for money in order for the rest of the family to survive. Three men and a woman face 12 years in prison after travelling from Vietnam to China, trafficking 19 people to go and sell their kidneys. University and college students are turning to prostitution in order to make ends meet and pay off their school fees.

Today, there is no place around the globe where crime is not on the increase. This is not helped by the increasing availability of drugs and alcohol. Places which hitherto had been safe haven have become crime spots for muggings, burglary, shootings, and knife crimes. Elderly people are being murdered in their homes by drug addicts looking for money for the next fix. Serial killers prowl the streets and neighbourhoods looking for their next victim, and organised criminals are unleashing their latest version and wave of cyber-crime.

There is a growing gang culture in many of our cities. Lawlessness is the order of the day. We live in a world where young lives are being taken by gangs and children are stabbed to death by criminals bent on stealing mobile phones. In London at the end of January 2013, a boy of 16 years begged for his life before he was killed by a mob of youths brandishing knives and swords. In many of our inner city estates, children as young as eleven years old act as watchers or look-outs, couriers and runners for drug warlords. It is unspoken and denied but there are many no-go areas for law enforcement agencies, unless they go en-masse. The result: ordinary law-abiding citizens live in fear, often reluctant or unable to leave their homes.

Towards the end of 2012, a young man of 20, but apparently suffering from autism, went into a school where his mother worked as an assistant, and shot dead primary school pupils and teachers in cold blood. The same man had shot dead his mother while in bed before proceeding on his killing spree. A few months before that, a masked gunman massacred 12 people and wounded 58 as they watched a midnight showing of the new Batman film – *The Dark Knight Rises* - in Denver Colorado, in July of 2012. A year before then, Anders Breivik killed 77 people at a ruling Labour Party youth camp in Utoya, in Norway.

Terrorist activities are on the increase. Many groups are now springing up in Africa - in areas where such activities were never heard of before. There is no let-up in civil wars in many regions around the world. As I write, the civil war in Syria has been on-going for close to three years. The nuclear threat around the world has never been greater. Politicians and public office holders in many parts of the world are busy looting the coffers of their nations, siphoning billions of dollars to secret accounts abroad, while their subjects wallow in abject poverty, suffering and ill-health.

The catalogue of events and problems, both local and global, which have been referred to, leave even the casual reader in no doubt that the world is in crisis. This crisis is man-made and totally avoidable. Someone has said, 'At the heart of the human problem is the problem of the human heart'. Greed, malice, perversion, idolatry, arrogance, deception and other forms of evil, all stem from within each of us.

How then do we tackle these mammoth problems? Obviously, this is a logical question to ask. We will seek to address that question in the succeeding chapters. The first thing we need to do is to accept that there is a problem or that we are facing a crisis of global proportions. Acceptance that there is a problem makes you want to look for a solution. However, the point of divergence for many comes when seeking to identify the root causes, as exemplified by the difference of opinion between Prime Minster David Cameron and former Premier, Tony Blair, regarding the reasons for the August 2011 riots across Britain's cities.

The Bible shows us that the historic and current human malaise is not caused by material, financial, or socio-economic factors. The root cause is spiritual. There are those who may wish to join issues over this. The biblical position is very clear: the ills, ailments and afflictions of life stem from man's rejection of the loving rule of our Creator-God who has revealed Himself through His Son Jesus Christ. He offers us a way out of our misery and misplaced priorities. There is a prescribed way with God and that there is also a proscribed way that He disapproves of.

The experience of Isaac, the central character of this book is a universal case study of how to respond to life's issues and challenges. His story begins with this foreboding statement: *'Now there was a famine in the land, besides the previous famine that had occurred in the days of Abraham (26:1a).* This was a big problem for him. Everything he had acquired in life was at risk. He could lose everything. He was in the land that God had promised Abraham his father and his descendants, yet here was this huge threat. How could that possibly be? That was not what God promised his father, you might say.

Unfortunately, there are many Christians who expect a trouble-free stroll through their Christian life. Exacting and unpleasant circumstances are not part of their theology. They think that God's blessings can be seen by observing which group of people are having it good and which ones are having it bad. Sometimes when tests and trials come to us, we are disheartened and think that God has abandoned us. Let me encourage you, **faith grows in the face of adversity.** Hardship has the capacity not only to strengthen us but draw us closer to God. God's pattern is to allow and use adversity to mould us on the pathway to prosperity.

When you read through the Bible, you will find that there are no less than 13 famines mentioned. The first is found in Genesis 12:10. It took place during Abraham's life time. So, even though Isaac was exactly where God wanted Him to be, the place of promised blessing had become a risky, threatening and dangerous environment. Isaac probably was still living at Beer Lahai Roi (Genesis 25:11) when the famine struck. The famine posed a threat to him and his family. He was faced with the same kind of problem that his father Abraham had faced: a lack of rain and its severe impact on crops and animals. He moved to Gerar, which was in Philistine country, probably because the famine was less severe there. We don't know for sure; some suggest that it was closer to the coast than his place of abode.

Isaac's secondary problem was a bi-product of his prosperity. There was hostility, rooted in jealousy, from his Philistine neighbours, aroused by his growing wealth - at a time of famine. Today, that famine is represented not only by the current economic recession, but the increasing multi-faceted problems and challenges that are trying to tear apart the fabric of modern society and the very essence of life on earth as God originally intended it. Note this very important point: some people will celebrate you; others will tolerate you, and the rest will hate you. It matters not; what matters most is your relationship with God and His unconditional love for you.

At the risk of stating the blindingly obvious, when we look at Isaac's experience and life in general we come to one important conclusion: that the journey towards recovery always begins with a crisis. Permit me to explain. Here is another seemingly obvious statement: if there is no problem there would be no need for a recovery. A crisis therefore is a solution that is incubating, waiting to emerge or be found.

Timeless Truths

- The journey towards recovery always begins with a crisis.

- The ills, ailments, and afflictions of life stem from man's rejection of the loving rule of our Creator-God.

- Acceptance that there is a problem makes you want to look for a solution.

- Faith grows in the face of adversity.

- Hardship has the capacity not only to strengthen us but draw us closer to God.

Chapter 2

YOU NEED REVELATION

*The Lord appeared to Isaac and said, "Do not go down
to Egypt; live in the land where I tell you to live. Stay in
this land for a while, and I will be with you and will bless
you. For to you and your descendants I will give all these
lands and will confirm the oath I swore to your father
Abraham. I will make your descendants as numerous as the
stars in the sky and will give them all these lands,
and through your offspring all nations on earth will be
blessed, because Abraham obeyed me and did everything I
required of him, keeping my commands, my decrees
and my instructions."*
(Genesis 26:2-5)

WHERE or to whom do you turn in search of answers
to life's problems? Where do you run to when
danger threatens you and your family? Where do
you look for ideas and a way out? Many turn to friends,
trusted allies, mentors or advisers; whilst others rely on
themselves, their acquired knowledge and experience. The
sad truth is that decisions are reached and choices made

17

without reference to God, often with disastrous consequences.

The human race is at a critical crossroad. The choices we make as individuals, families, corporations, and communities will have a lasting impact on the generations yet to be born. Everywhere you turn, there is pressure; pressure at home and abroad, in the workplace, in the family, in relationships, in business and in community life. There is pressure to give up and throw in the towel. There is pressure to be or not to be, pressure to conform or not to conform, pressure from superiors as well as peers, pressure to stay and pressure to run away. What is clear from the Bible and the experience of those who have lived the Bible way is that times of pressure are God's way of getting our attention. It is therefore vital that we pause, listen carefully, making sure that we have heard from God, before proceeding further in dealing with the current predicament we find ourselves in. The problem however is that people have a tendency to ignore the elephant in the room, preferring to lean towards the easy, the novel or the superficial; rather than focus on the key issue and follow timeless principles to deal with the challenges they are faced with.

One of the difficulties we face, especially in social groups is one of trying to agree upon a shared understanding of the issue confronting us. I call this the 'problem of alignment'. Due to our individual make up, the influences on us and interest groups we represent, different people see things differently. As a consequence a shared definition of the problem is often difficult and sometimes impossible. The truth is that without an agreed definition of the real issue, there cannot be a move to the next step of searching for possible solutions and the appropriate actions to take in order to address the issue.

In a group setting, the first task is to clearly define and agree what the problem is. Only then can a search for the right solution begin. In Isaac's case, defining the problem was not an issue. The issue was how he should respond to the problem confronting him. This is the second step in the process. This brings us to the very heart of the first step on the road to recovery – a revelation of what to do. Isaac's experience teaches us that we need a clear and specific word from God as to what to do.

Understanding the realities of God's self-revelation

The Bible shows us that it is in these places or seasons of crises that God shows up, reveals Himself, or helps us to see a relevant aspect of His nature and character. More often than not, it is also in times of crisis that we are most ready to hear from God – when we have reached the end of our tether, our self-will crushed and our puny efforts reduced to rubble. It is when we are seemingly helpless, broken by the buffetings of life, that we are ready for the intervention of God. It all begins with a crisis, and I will consider a well-known example from the Bible.

One day an Israelite who had been raised in the courts of Pharaoh, King of Egypt, was walking by and saw an Egyptian mistreating an Israelite. The man intervened and killed the Egyptian. Fearing he was going to be executed by Pharaoh for the murder, the man ran away to the land of Midian, where he married and raised children. That man's name is

Moses. Whilst in exile, Moses, a man who had been raised a prince, worked for his father-in-law as a shepherd. Moses was 40 years old when he committed the murder. The next 40 years had passed and he was now 80 years of age. It seemed that life had passed him by and that he was going to continue his job as a lowly shepherd through to retirement. One day, all that changed.

Moses was tending the flock of Jethro, his father-in-law, the priest of Midian. While at Horeb, he had an encounter that radically changed the course of his life. There he was, an 80-year-old man, well past pensionable age, still working when most people would have retired. All of a sudden, he was confronted by an incredible sight and sound. An angel of God appeared to him in a flaming fire in the middle of a bush. The bush was burning, but the bush was not burnt by the fire. Moses turned to look at this unusual sight. As he did, God spoke to him: 'Moses, Moses'. His response was, 'Here I am'. God said to Him: (i) Take your sandals off, because the place you are standing is holy ground; (ii) 'I *am* the God of your father – the God of Abraham, the God of Isaac, and the God of Jacob.'

These words of instruction and revelation from God to Moses are significant. Yes, the ground that Moses was standing was holy. That however was not the only reason why God told him to take off his shoes. Taking off your shoe is a sign of yielding your rights to live your life exactly as you want. It is a sign of the abandonment of pride. It is also a sign of submission and yielding to God's authority; a sign of respect.

Second, the expression, '...God of Abraham, the God of

Isaac, and the God of Jacob', is more than a literary motif. God was re-affirming to Moses His character as a covenant-making, covenant-keeping God, who watches over His Word to ensure that it is fulfilled. There is context, consistency and continuity. God was in effect saying that what He did in the life of each of the three patriarchs He is able to do in the life of the nation of Israel.

Moses hid his face because of fear of looking at God's face. God went on: (iii) I have seen the oppression of my people. I have heard their cry because of the affliction of their Egyptian taskmasters and know their sorrows. I have come down to deliver them. God went on: (iv) I want to send you, Moses, to Pharaoh, to bring my people Israel, out of Egypt.

I want you to put yourself in Moses' position. What would be your reaction? Moses' reaction was: 'You can't be serious, God. You've got the wrong man. I have a great idea: why don't you give my brother Aaron a call?' Moses raised five different objections (some say excuses) as to why he was unsuited for the task (Exodus 3:11; 3:13; 4:1; 4:10; 4:13). First, who am I that I should go? (Exodus 3:11). Second, what is your name, so that I can tell them? (Exodus 3:13). Third, the people won't believe me or listen to me (Exodus 4:1). Fourth, I am slow of speech, and not eloquent enough (Exodus 4:10). Fifth, send someone else! (Exodus 4:13).

I am most interested in the second of Moses' five objections: 'What is your name, so I can tell them?' God gave a rather unusual response (Exodus 3:14-15): *God said to Moses, "I AM who I AM. This is what you are to say to the Israelites: 'I AM has sent me to you.'" God also said to Moses, "Say to the Israelites, 'The LORD, the God of your fathers—the God of Abraham, the God of Isaac and the God of Jacob—has sent me to you.' This is my name forever, the name you shall call me from generation to generation."*

Remember, God had called, and was in the process of commissioning Moses to go back to Egypt. Moses is feeling rather exposed and vulnerable. He was an 80-year-old lowly shepherd who had been out of Egypt for 40 years. He felt he had lost his edge and was afraid of being asked a theological question. What would happen if the people tested him to see if he was credible and ticked all the boxes? How was he going to answer them or cope? All these thoughts must have run through his mind. So, he raised an objection. Moses pleaded lack of knowledge. He was saying that he did not even know God's name and had no idea what to tell the Israelites.

Moses had been in a crisis for 40 years. He was a criminal on the run. The people of Israel were also in crisis. They were in bondage and were being brutalised by their Egyptian masters. God appeared to an 80-year-old murderer and gave him an assignment that took him way outside his comfort zone. Moses was in the place of revelation. A fugitive was about to be sent on an assignment that took him back to the scene of his criminal past and to the authorities who had been looking for him all these years.

Revelation is radically different from information. The former comes from God, whilst the latter is from the earth. Revelation is God's word to man, whilst information is man's word to man. Information is readily available (just Google it), **revelation is however a gracious gift from God**. The purpose of revelation is to transform our lives for the better (not necessarily making us happier), but above all, to advance God's kingdom.

God gave Moses an answer, saying, 'I am that I am', 'I am who I am' or 'I am who I say I am'. In 21ˢᵗ century Western culture, personal names are little more than labels we use to distinguish one person from another. In many cases the names are just a meaningless jumble of letters. In the Hebrew culture, a name is more than a title. It denotes and signifies the essence of who that person is or is expected to be. Generally speaking, the African concept of names is similar to the Hebrew. In the Hebrew (and African) culture, a name would speak of family, local community or clan history. It would signify identity, ancestry, project, hopes, dreams, desires and aspirations. A name carried special significance; it was a sign of authority and power. Names are often prophetic; a person's name identified them and stood for something specific. This is especially true of God.

In the Bible, God changed the names of many people - Abram to Abraham, Sarai to Sarah, and Jacob to Israel, thus altering or re-aligning their destiny to His purpose. So, like Hebrew names, the name of God is more than a mere title. It represents His divine nature or character, and His relationship with His people. The names of God are like miniature portraits and promises. God's name represents the deity as He is known to those who encounter and worship Him. God's name reveals His identity, His authority, His activity, His power, His presence, His majesty, and His position.

So, when God gives a new manifestation of His interest or care, it gives rise to a new name. This is how it works: when someone encounters God in a particular area of need in their life, that person recognises and calls God by that name. For example, if that person has been miraculously healed, then God in their experience becomes the miraculous healer. Also, an old name may acquire new content and significance through new and varied experiences of these sacred relations and encounters that God's people have with Him.

What then was God telling Moses to say to the people? 'I am that I am', literally translates as: 'I will be that which I now am', or 'I will be what I will be' – (Hebrew – 'Ehyeh Asher Ehyeh'). However, in most English Bibles, this phrase is rendered as, 'I am that I am'. In the Torah, the Jewish Bible, the term YHWH, pronounced in English as YAHWEH, the Hebrew name for God, appears 6518 times. This number in itself is quite remarkable compared with titles given to God, namely: God (2,605), Almighty (48), Lord (40), Maker (25), Creator (7), Father (7), Ancient of Days (3) and Grand Instructor (2).

God was saying: I am *Yahweh* (YHWH), which comes from a verb which means 'to exist, be.' Put another way, it means: 'He who is self-existing, self-sufficient,' or, more concretely, 'He who lives'. 'I am that I am' stresses God as the independent and self-existent God of revelation and redemption. God was saying, 'I am the living God', in contrast to the lifeless gods of the heathen. 'I am the source and author of life'. In other words, 'If you want life, I, the living God can give it to you. I am who I am. I will be what I will be. I am He who lives.' God is saying, 'I am uncreated. I stand alone. I am on-going. I do not die. I cannot die'. God told Moses to say to the children of Israel: *'God said to Moses, "I AM WHO I AM. This is what you are to say to the Israelites: 'I AM has sent me to you.'"'*.

It begs the question, "What is that which God is and has been?"

We get further indication of what God was saying to Moses in Exodus 3:15:

God also said to Moses, "Say to the Israelites, 'The Lord, the God of your fathers — the God of Abraham, the God of Isaac and the God of Jacob — has sent me to you.' This is my name forever, the name you shall call me from generation to generation."

Having said, 'I am the self-existent One; I am Yahweh; I am who I am', God goes on to elaborate and point them to their history. He said, *'I am the God of Abraham, Isaac and Jacob'.* How then did God reveal or show Himself to these three patriarchs? What lessons are there for us?

Abram and Abraham's God – Our God

Abram had many moments of crises and difficulties throughout his life. For a hundred years there was one major crisis: he had no child, no one to succeed him and carry on his name. So, how did God show Himself? At key moments in Abram's walk, God revealed Himself as: the God who calls (Genesis 12:1-3); the God who makes covenant (eternal, unmerited, life-changing, destiny-defining promises (Genesis 12:1-3); the God who makes and keeps His covenant (Genesis 15:7-21); God Almighty (Genesis 17:1). The Hebrew expression is El Shaddai (God Almighty) means that God has all might or all power and as such He can do all things. Everything is possible with God; God provides (Genesis 22); He is the everlasting God (Genesis 21:33).

God's revelation in times of crisis is multi-faceted. In times of lack, He appeared and still appears as Jehovah-Jireh – "*the*

Lord will provide" (Genesis 22:13, 14). In times of sickness, He comes as Jehovah-Rapha – *"the Lord that heals"* (Exodus 15:26). In the midst of conflict and the battle of your life, He is Jehovah-Nissi – *"the Lord our banner"* (Exodus 17:8-15). If you are troubled, within and without, He is Jehovah-Shalom – *"the Lord our peace,"* or *"the Lord send peace"* (Judges 6:24). If you are drifting without anchor or direction in life, He is Jehovah-Ra-ah – *"the Lord my shepherd"* (Psalm 23). In our sin-soaked, filthy-rag condition, He is Jehovah-Tsidkenu – *"the Lord our righteousness"* (Jeremiah 23:6). If you are feeling abandoned and all alone, He is Jehovah-Shammah – *"the Lord is present"* (Ezekiel 48:35). Jehovah-Shammah signifies Jehovah's abiding presence with His people (Exodus 33:14, 15; Psalm 16:11, 97:5; Matthew 28:20; Hebrews 13:5). So the first thing you must have is a revelation of who God is; otherwise you will wander, worry or misconstrue His intentions for your life.

God's revelation to Isaac

How did God relate to Isaac especially in his moment of crisis? First, you need to note that Isaac was not the only inhabitant in the land. The land was populated by other people: families, clans, high born, lowly born, rich and poor. They all faced the same issue – famine. National or regional problems, especially those associated with the weather system, very often don't discriminate. The rich, even in their mansions, also cry. For example, in 2011, a 9.0 magnitude earthquake resulted in an equally powerful tsunami that struck the eastern coastline of Japan, causing the death of 19,000 people. The disaster did not distinguish between rich and poor.

Second, famine was not a new phenomenon; it happened in Abraham's days. Third, it was God who took the initiative to communicate with Isaac. There are numerous occasions in the Bible when people approached God out of their own volition. In this instance however, as in many others, it was God who made the first move. This is not surprising, and I would like to submit two reasons for that. First, God must have seen the condition of Isaac's heart. He was debating what to do. God knew what was best for Isaac and so came and spoke to him. God, who is all-knowing, did not want Isaac to follow in his father's footsteps and head for Egypt. We will look at this in more detail in the next two chapters.

In the meantime, here is a summary of what God said to Isaac. First, do not go down to Egypt. Second, stay or live in the land that I am going to show you. Third, I will be with you. Fourth, I will bless you. Fifth, I will give you and your descendants the inheritance I promised to Abraham your father. God showed Himself as One who directs and guides; the God who makes promises; the God who is faithful; the God who multiplies seeds and gives a rich harvest in the midst of a famine. This was not the first time Isaac heard the voice of God. He was present on Mount Moriah (Genesis 22:9-18) many years before, when God held back the hand of his father, Abraham, from offering him, Isaac, as a sacrifice. This time, instead of being the second major character, Isaac was the only character as God spoke to him personally and directly. God deliberately revealed Himself to Isaac in the face of a major dilemma.

Revelation is a supernatural download of God's mind from heaven to man, for direction, guidance, encourage-

ment, strength, support, protection, and blessing. Revelation is ultimately for the fulfilment of His agenda for the world, individuals, families, people, groups or nations. There is no 'one-size-fits-all' when it comes to hearing from God. God gives us revelation based on our need and His purposes. There are many response options open to us in a crisis situation. You can take the fatalist's approach and do nothing – whatever will be will be, follow your natural instincts, or man's rational ideas; tread the well-worn path of experience by doing what you have always done in the past; or you can seek a word, a clear vision or revelation from God.

I never cease to be amazed at the extent to which individuals, families, communities and nations will go in an attempt to fix the crises in their lives, sometimes even when it is manifestly self-evident that they have no idea what the cause of the problem is. Isaac faced the same issue as his father, Abram. There was a famine in the land. The natural response for Isaac was to run away, taking what seemed to be the path of least resistance, the way that most people would go. This is the highway of the masses, the expressway of the multitudes. More often than not it leads to a dead end or proves disastrous.

In the face of famine Abram had chosen to leave the land to which God had led him, in order to go down to Egypt. God's mercy preserved Abram. However, for Isaac not to go with the flow of the crowd, his own natural instincts, or preference for flight, he needed a word: a clear revelation, and a directive from God. God appeared to Isaac and spoke to him very clearly: 'Stay in this land; don't run away to Egypt.' Revelation is required in all aspects of your life if you have to move forward and recover, be it spiritual, moral, social, financial, marital or political. In the midst of your own crisis, you too need a revelation from God.

God wants each one of us to be recipients and carriers of revelation. Re-discovering the place of revelation and moving in it is one of the keys to total recovery and prosperity. The seed of God's blessing is the Word received by faith. Abraham is a perfect example. When there was a dispute between his herdsmen and those of his nephew, Lot, he avoided a quarrel by allowing Lot to choose which part of the land to live. He knew that the promise of God was to him and wherever he went that word of promise travelled with him (Genesis 13:5-18). That word was resident in Abraham and Isaac, and as they obeyed what God had said to them, it would be fulfilled. It did not matter where they were, the promised blessing would be seen in their lives. The promise of blessing to Abram was in relation to the land that he occupied and not in Egypt where he went in search of economic survival. Your provision is in God's Word, and you therefore need to hear what He is saying specifically about what you should do now.

The situation with Isaac was particularly dire. There was famine in the land and things were hard. Conditions were tough and the temptation was there to run away, but God appeared to Him. He not only appeared, He spoke to him and told him specifically not to go down to Egypt to live. God said to Isaac: "I will be with you; I will bless you; I will give you and your descendants the inheritance that I promised to Abraham your father." The intention of God was very clear, as can be seen in the words He spoke. God still speaks today through His Word and prophetically, through those who are committed to hearing from Him. You must therefore decide to listen, discern, decode and obey what He has said.

The problem sometimes with us human beings is that we think we have the answers; but often we forget that things are never exactly the way they seem. What might make sense rationally may not necessarily be part of God's will for those who follow Jesus as Saviour and Lord. There is always that risk of acting against the will of God, particularly when you don't take care to ask Him for direction. Abram went down to Egypt when God did not tell him to go. He did not first ask God what to do before making his move. So, the message here is simple: in the midst of your issues and challenges, make sure to constantly tune in to the divine wavelength, to hear and receive specific revelation and direction as to what to do.

This is what the LORD says:

"Stand at the crossroads and look; ask for the ancient paths, ask where the good way is, and walk in it, and you will find rest for your souls. But you said, 'We will not walk in it.' (Jeremiah 6:16).

You may ask: "What then are the ancient paths?" These are the principles, truths and patterns that are rooted in God's Word - revealed specifically to you, and tailor-made for your unique situation. Our examination of Genesis 26 and the examples we saw at the beginning of the book depict how these principles are apt for today. The treasures of wisdom are there for us. All we need to do is to desire, ask, seek and we shall find. You need to seek and discover the ancient paths. You will prosper and recover if you follow them. Once you understand these principles, you must engage in honest dialogue with yourself, not so you can indulge in self-pity, blame yourself or find a scapegoat, but so you can align yourself with God's Word, searching for practical solutions, as you pray, work and continue to look for results.

God wants to bring you and me to a place of yielding and responding to Him in humility. But unfortunately, man today wants to do his own thing; and leave God behind in their lives and decision-making. Humans tend to ignore the *elephant* in the room, preferring to lean towards things that are easy, novel, and superficial, instead of focusing on the key issues and following timeless principles that are directly linked to the real problems or challenges confronting them. Even more worrying is the fact that when God has issued a clear directive or instruction, human beings want to do the exact opposite, and having done so, wonder why things are not working. But God is saying: "*Guys, no matter how sophisticated or advanced you think you are, I am still God. I do not change, and I won't compromise My ways for yours. What you need to do is to go back to the ancient paths.*"

What is clear to see is that people have profound difficulties facing the real issue, or the actions that they need to take in order to deal with the problem. However, the call today is for alignment. This begins with hearing God's *Rhema* or 'now' word, seeing the future as He sees it and following His direction. In order to recover as individuals, families, organisations, communities, movements and denominations, we must start the re-digging of the ancient wells for a better, greater and more prosperous future. It is about re-discovering and recovering lost things. We must go back to the foundations; we must return to scriptural principles and keys that will lead us to a more prosperous future.

Timeless Truths

- Names are often prophetic; a person's name identified them and stood for something specific. This is especially true of God.

- Revelation from God is given for direction, guidance, encouragement, strength, support, protection and blessing of man.

- Revelation from God is ultimately for the fulfilment of God's agenda for the world.

Chapter 3

RECEIVING AND WALKING
IN REVELATION

In the same way, you who are younger, submit yourselves to your elders. All of you, clothe yourselves with humility toward one another, because, "God opposes the proud but shows favour to the humble.' Humble yourselves, therefore, under God's mighty hand, that he may lift you up in due time.
(1 Peter 5:5-6)

W E have already touched on what revelation is. **It is God's disclosure of His will and purpose for our benefit and blessing and for the fulfilment of His eternal purpose.** How then do we access this revelation? In many ways it is not so much how we come by it; it is more about God coming to us to show us His thoughts. We cannot earn the right to revelation; like all things relating to God, it is all by His grace. It is totally unmerited, unearned and un-earnable. However, there are principles, postures, patterns, attitudes and mind-sets which we can follow to position ourselves in the place of hearing from God. Here are some basic disciplines that will help you in seeking the mind of God. I call these the eight 'As' (or 8 'As').

Ask

The word 'ask' itself is the acronym for *Ask, Seek,* and *Knock*. We are currently living in the post information age - the shift age - where information changes rapidly, and is made available on all sorts of platforms. The temptation with the great advance in technology is to assume that you have answers to everything at your fingertips or that you have your hand firmly on every pulse, or even worse, to pretend that you have everything under your control. But the reality is that a common sense approach to the root problem facing the world today has only yielded common results. It is high time we asked the Lord for help, and return to the ancient pathways.

The Bible says:

> *"Ask and it will be given to you; seek and you will find; knock and the door will be opened to you.*
> *(Matthew 7:7)*

In asking we must seek intimacy with God through prayer and purity. Both intimacy and humility are acknowledgments of our total dependence on God. It is an open declaration that we do not have the answers and that apart from Him we can do nothing. It is the place of vulnerability where we seek to connect with the Divine mind. We must study the Word of God and ask the Holy Spirit to enable us to find the hidden treasure in the Word.

Above

You must realise that your help is from 'above', and I mean from God, and no one else. Every effort of man without the help of God will only end in futility or frustration. God may use people or circumstances for His agenda but ultimately, the source of your help is from Him. It is important to state this clearly, so that while searching for revelation, you don't start to look in the wrong places. When a man is in trouble or difficulty, everyone and everything looks like the solution. If you have ever been in a position where you have become very hungry, and I mean really hungry, everything starts looking and smelling like bread to you. You may also have been in a situation, say for instance when you have decided to buy a car and have finally settled on the make and model. Very quickly, you will discover that you start to see that type of car everywhere and anywhere you go. The truth is: everyone and everything cannot provide you with life's solutions, and that is why you must be sensitive to God's leading, so that you don't make a wrong choice. The same is true about revelation; unless it is from God, recovery cannot be guaranteed. True revelation comes from above.

The Psalmist says:

'I lift up my eyes to the mountains— where does my help come from? My help comes from the Lord, the Maker of heaven and earth.' (Psalm 121:1-2)

'I sought the Lord, and he answered me; he delivered me from all my fears. Those who look to him are radiant; their faces are never covered with shame. This poor man called, and the Lord heard him; he saved him out of all his troubles.' (Psalm 34:4-6)

Ancient

Many people in the world today wish God could change His ways to accommodate their wishes, preferences, excesses, and so called alternative lifestyles. Christianity and Christian values are attacked as being traditional, narrow, not inclusive, and outmoded in our modern age. Ancient is a word that is not often used. There is an unstated assumption that anything that is old, traditional or long-standing is irrelevant and useless, even downright offensive or wrong. Nothing could be further from the truth. Truth applies universally through every age, time and season. Its eternal and universal applicability is the very essence of its authority. The Word of God is settled for ever and cannot change. God Himself is unchangeable and He has set this life in motion and existence according to His patterns and principles. The ancient texts which continue to speak to us through the ages are immutable in principle and dynamic in operation. It is man that must change, align with the will and ways of God, in order to recover from our current predicament.

Alignment

You can get revelation from God but unless you align your will with Him, God's intended blessings for your life will not materialise. You must align with His person, and by this, you must believe that He is the Giver of life and the repository of all knowledge and wisdom. You must also connect with His Spirit, as God is Spirit. You do this by asking. It is part of the process of humbling yourself before an Almighty God. It is not great for human pride but wonderful for the soul. It is necessary because the natural man does not understand the things of God, and if you must connect with God and flow at the same frequency, you need to ask Him to help you.

Jesus said those who worship God must worship Him in spirit and in truth. The word 'worship' here does not only mean 'worship' the way we commonly view it today. It begins with an understanding of who God is. That understanding leads us to come with a sense of readiness of mind and heart, submission, reverence, awe, openness and wonder, with a deep desire to honour God as God. God's Word is truth. That means we come with our hearts submitted to the Word of God.

Alignment is obedience and submission to God's Word. This is fundamentally an issue of authority. The story of the centurion in Matthew 8:5-13 illustrates this point very clearly. Here was a man of authority who understood the principles of authority. He came to Jesus to seek for help on behalf of his sick servant. He knew that Jesus had greater power. By his very words, the centurion was in effect subjecting himself to the authority of Jesus. By doing so, he was also aligning himself with the flow of divine authority. His humility set a direct connecting wire between the words of Jesus and his sick servant, who as we know was healed instantly. That is what happens when you align yourself with revelation from God – you recover.

Approach

If you are looking for revelation from God you have to approach Him with a paradoxical combination of reverence and awe, allied to boldness. We see this again in the story of Jesus' encounter with the leper (Matthew 8:1-4, Mark 1:40-45 and Luke 5:12-16.) and the centurion (Matthew 8:5-13). Both came with these two qualities, yet expressed them in different ways. The centurion came humbly, and by faith, confident that Jesus could and would heal his servant. On the other hand, the leper came humbly, but there was something different about his mind-set. Whilst he believed Jesus could heal him, otherwise he would not have come, what he doubted was Jesus' willingness to do so. It is never a question of whether the Lord was able but a question of whether He was willing. That was why he said, 'Lord, if you are willing'.

Whilst like the centurion, the leper came with reverence and awe, there appears to be certain timidity about the leper. With the understanding of how authority works, the centurion boldly asked Jesus to make a verbal declaration about his sick servant. In contrast, the leper doubted Jesus' willingness. Our approach must exude boldness (Hebrews 4:16), not in an attitude of familiarity, but one of reverence and awe. A wrong approach to God blocks revelation and prevents recovery.

You must also approach God with sincerity of purpose – to obtain light to illuminate certain aspects of life in order to move forward. Some people today seek knowledge and information to add to the bank of 'insights' they already have - to impress, to cajole, and even to confuse others without necessarily wanting to change anything for the better. You can fool men but must also realise that God searches the heart to give to everyone according to what is in their heart. The Bible puts this succinctly as follows:

I the LORD search the heart and examine the mind, to reward each person according to their conduct, according to what their deeds deserve." (Jeremiah 17:10, NIV)

Attitude

You may have heard the saying that 'It is your attitude that determines your altitude in life'. It is your attitude to receiving the revelation of God on a particular issue that determines the depth of insights and the breadth of your understanding. The fundamental attitude required is one of humility. This is the very essence of Christ, who was humble to the point of dying on the Cross for our sins. Humility is accepting that we cannot help ourselves, and being sensible enough, to look for and accept help from the One who is able to deliver man from all circumstances.

The Bible says:

'Humble yourselves before the Lord, and he will lift you up. (James 4:10)

In the same way, you who are younger, submit yourselves to your elders. All of you, clothe yourselves with humility toward one another, because, "God opposes the proud but shows favour to the humble.' Humble yourselves, therefore, under God's mighty hand, that he may lift you up in due time. (1 Peter 5:5-6)

Then one of the synagogue leaders, named Jairus, came, and when he saw Jesus, he fell at his feet. He pleaded earnestly with him, "My little daughter is

*dying. Please come and put your hands on her so that
she will be healed and live." (Mark 5:22-23)*

The above scriptures speak for themselves: humility and
being teachable are necessary to receive revelation, and when
you follow the truth that these verses teach, you position
yourself for revelation and blessing from God.

Acceptance

God's Word or revelation is final. When God speaks, our role
is to listen and obey. The revelation from God concerning
what to do in order to recover from any given situation can
only be for your benefit. His ways and thoughts are radically
different and diametrically opposed to that of man. His
verdict on an issue is final. Once you receive a revelation,
write it down, being clear about what you have received.
Also, believe it, take hold of it, and let it take hold of you
through meditation and prayer, regardless of the outlook or
the negative circumstances that may surround you.

Once in ancient Israel, in the northern kingdom known as
Samaria, there was a siege which brought about a serious
famine in the land. Things were so bad that cannibalism was
practised and people were living on bird droppings. Elisha
the prophet came on the scene and declared that there would
be abundance of food within 24 hours. To the natural mind
that was impossible. Indeed the king's most trusted advisor
openly challenged the prophet's declaration. In response, the
prophet told the advisor that he would hear and see the
promised abundance but would not eat of it. The prophet's
word was fulfilled on both counts. The siege was broken,

there was surplus food, and the king's chief advisor was trampled at the gates following a stampede of the masses as they rushed out of the city to gather the food and other spoils of victory. **Yours is not to do the mathematics when it comes to the word of God; your main responsibility is to believe and obey.**

Application

A lot of people have received revelation from God about their recovery. These people already have knowledge. However, they have done nothing with it. They keep wishing that something would dramatically change in their lives. But to their surprise, nothing has changed. The answer is simple: step out in obedience to the word that you have already received. Like Isaac, you must walk in the revelation, the knowledge, and the faith you have; taking simple steps forward in line with God's word to you. As you do so, you will experience recovery.

The Church of Jesus Christ is also called to walk in revelation and apply godly principles rather than being swayed by the tide of public opinion. The first century Church moved in apostolic conviction and prophetic revelation. The process was that God spoke, apostles moved in faith (apostolic conviction), and things happened, as God honoured His word and their faith (obedience). Prophetic revelation, apostolic conviction, and apostolic immediacy were the three key drivers of the rapid growth of the early Church. That simple formula was consistently evident throughout the book of Acts. For example, in Acts 9, we see the conversion and baptism of Saul of Tarsus. In Acts 10, we have the visions of Peter and the supernatural connection with Cornelius. Again, in Acts 13:1-3, Apostle Paul and Barnabas were called and commissioned into missionary service. The revelation which they received brought fresh impetus to the mission of the infant Church, which in turn led to the visible extension of the footprints of Christ's kingdom into Europe.

What is clear from Isaac's experience and many others in the Bible and life in general, is that times of pressure or crises are God's way of getting our attention, calling us to remember, repent and return, and bringing us to a place of yielding and responding to Him in humility. As He did with Isaac, God will often use adversity and opposition to lead us back to the place of His promise and presence. The implication is that we need to seek and discover the ancient paths – principles, truths and patterns – that are rooted in God's Word, revealed specifically to us, and tailor-made for our unique situation. If we follow them, we will definitely prosper. I am speaking here about prosperity in the holistic sense of the word as it appears in the Bible. As we shall see later, as we explore further the life of Isaac, true prosperity flows from the very heart of our relationship with God. It is fundamentally spiritual and supernatural, transcending the material and touching every facet of life.

Timeless Truths

- The place of asking is the place of vulnerability where we seek to connect with the Divine mind.

- It is in the place or season of crisis that God reveals or helps us to see a relevant aspect of His nature and character.

- More often than not it is in times of crisis that we are most ready to hear from God.

- Revelation is a gracious gift from God aimed at transforming our lives for the better and to advance His purposes.

- Yours is not to do the mathematics when it comes to the word of God; your main responsibility is to believe and obey.

Chapter 4

STAY IN THE LAND

The LORD appeared to Isaac and said, "Do not go down to Egypt; live in the land where I tell you to live. Stay in this land for a while. (...) So Isaac stayed in Gerar. Then Abimelek said to Isaac, "Move away from us; you have become too powerful for us." So Isaac moved away from there and encamped in the Valley of Gerar, where he settled. (Genesis 26:2-3a, 6, 16-17)

THE 'flight or fight' response is a natural instinct that God has endowed humans and animals with. When your life, livelihood, status, position, or personal integrity is threatened, the most natural thing you want to do is to fight back or to escape. I have seen this in friendship and marriage relationships, in business, in times of natural disaster or periods of shifts in the economic landscape. The mass migrations in history have been driven by economic conditions. The harvest failed due to severe climatic changes. Obviously there are times when you have to move to escape adverse circumstances, environment, or situation. If you move without hearing clearly from God, you might get yourself into even more trouble.

The massive population shifts in and around the Horn of Africa over the last thirty years - starting with the famine in Ethiopia in the early 1980s, which spawned the Bob Geldof-led Band Aid - bear testimony to this very issue of fight or flight. There are situations when common sense dictates that one has to move. Remaining in the same place is simply waiting for the inevitable moment of death, which might be horrifically slow but certain. The old saying, 'he who fights and runs away lives to fight another day' applies. In many ways it is not a case of fighting; it is one of quickly taking to one's heels to reach a better place, in order to preserve life.

In areas of the world with tropical climates, the mass movement of people is either because the rains failed to come in due season, or some other natural disaster, such as crop disease. In more temperate climes, the Irish potato famine in the middle of the nineteenth century led to great suffering and massive movement of people, the result of which can be seen by the fact that today there are more people of Irish descent living in the USA than in Ireland itself.

What then do you do when things are not going as planned? What do you do when the expected progress is not being seen? What do you do when the environment has changed, or has become more hostile? What do you do when your dream is slowly turning into a nightmare?

When life is hard a number of suggestions and options may look appealing. Many advisers will come, readily offering you their services for free. Pro bono consultants will crawl out of the woodwork; self-appointed experts and ministers without portfolio will emerge in their mass ranks. Their counsel will come thick and fast. You will be advised to move from Jaipur to Johannesburg. You will be put under pressure to up sticks from Turkey to Tanzania. You will be persuaded to relocate from Niger to New Zealand. You will be encouraged to sell up, leave your wife and children and your extended family to a new found land, regardless of what might be awaiting you there. These advisers talk up the positives and discount the negatives. Success stories are cited, whilst failures and similar disasters go unmentioned or are glossed over. The reality however is that the grass is not always greener.

I originate from a part of the world where many of its citizens have emigrated to far regions of the earth; invariably away from their well-paid jobs, their family, their social networks, and spiritual roots - all in the quest for a better life. The evidence shows that the better life they are seeking is predominantly economic. People are so desperate sometimes that they would even take flights to places unknown. These people leave everything that gives them peace, security and joy to look for *Nirvana,* only to find out that the elusive panacea for the soul doesn't exist anywhere on the planet. For some it pays off, but for others the move has led to problems, some so severe they include marital or mental breakdown and even death.

At the back end of 2012, it was reported that up to 10,000 people were heading to a mystical mountain in Bugarach, a tiny village of 189 people in southern France, in the belief that 'aliens' or *Unidentified Flying Objects* (UFOs) will whisk them to safety in 'another dimension' when the world ends on 21st of December 2012. The reality is that we are still here; the world did not end on that day; there were no UFOs. The Mayan calendar which has been predicting the end of the world failed spectacularly yet again. Unfortunately, for one man who fell to his death while climbing the mountain earlier in that year, his world came to a shuddering end before the predicted date. What point am I trying to make here? It is that the hardships of life have given rise to desperate measures - people are willing to go to great lengths in search of a better place and life, often without knowing where they are going.

Famine signifies lack of food. By a principle of application it could be the lack of anything – money, friendship, joy, peace, happiness, or love. God had spoken to Isaac and commanded him to remain in Gerar and not to go down to Egypt. The revelation or word that God gave to him is capped off with a reiteration of the covenant promise that God had made to his father, Abraham. Isaac faced a severe famine in the land, and for him, it was either fight or flight. God told him to stay. He stayed where God had commanded him.

To the human mind, staying in Gerar in time of famine is like skydiving without a parachute. Catastrophe beckoned. To the natural mind, what Isaac experienced was simply impossible. The land was dry and dead. It held little prospects for life, not even for the worst form of subsistence farming. Yet Isaac prospered. This was the very first time God had spoken in this way to Isaac personally. He not only recognised that it was God, he readily submitted to what God had told him. Following the principles of God's Word guarantees His presence, protection and provision. God can bless you whatever the situation, whether it is a terrible marriage, bad economy, horrible workplace, hostile people or discrimination of any kind.

Isaac shows each one of us that **the key to progress and success is obedience**. Instead of leaving the land, Isaac obeyed God, stayed and began to sow there. As he sowed, God blessed and prospered him, giving him a one hundred-fold increase when it came to harvest time. This equates to ten thousand (10,000%) per cent. That means for every pound invested, the return would be ten thousand pounds. That is what I call favour.

There were two keys to Isaac's success: his obedience to God and the fact that he tapped into an ancient resource, water, from wells that his father, Abraham, had previously dug many years before. Isaac also dug new wells. Many of us are languishing spiritually and economically because we have moved from the land. The 'land' represents the centre of God's will for our lives. There are three 'lands' we can live in when it comes to the will of God. The first 'land' is when we pitch tent in the devil's kingdom. Simply put, we are living right outside the will of God. We become bread and meat for the enemy. The second 'land' is God's permissive will. This is a place where though not ideal, something of God's grace and providence is able to reach us. The third 'land' is a place of God's perfect will. That was the place where Isaac stationed himself. To the human eye, there was very little that spoke of perfection where Isaac was. Yet from God's perspective it was perfect.

"For my thoughts are not your thoughts, neither are your ways my ways," declares the Lord. *'As the heavens are higher than the earth, so are my ways higher than your ways and my thoughts than your thoughts'. (Isaiah 55: 8-9)*

In ancient Palestine, as in our world today, famine, which is evidenced by the lack of water and hence food, was a constant threat. In the face of famine Abram chose to leave the land to which God had led him, to go down to Egypt. Although Abram's sojourn to Egypt was not God-led, in spite of this, God in His mercy preserved him. Also, it was famine in Judah that prompted Elimelech to take his wife Naomi and two sons, Mahlon and Chilion, down to Moab (Ruth 1:1-2) where he and his two sons died. Both Abraham and Elimelech responded to the crises they were facing in the way they knew best, but without seeking the will of God. They both paid a heavy price in their own way: Abram by the apparent disconnection of his intimate fellowship with God, his lies and deception, whilst Elimelech and his two sons perished in the very land that was to be their place of preservation.

God's word to Isaac was to remain in the land. He stayed in Gerar. He lived there. He put down roots. He did not try to hedge his bets. On the contrary, he took possession. Those familiar with the ancient cultures of the Middle East will know that the act of digging a well was very significant; legally and economically. For Isaac there was an added dimension. His well-digging had a deep spiritual meaning. Wells are dug on one's land. Wells established rights of ownership. Anyone who dug a well was visibly laying claim to that piece of real estate and communicating that fact to those around. Isaac therefore stayed in the land – legally, economically, and above all spiritually.

In the process of time Isaac grew wealthy. His neighbours, the Philistines, became jealous and angry and felt threatened by his growing prosperity. How could he be doing so well when there was a famine in the land, whilst they in contrast, were struggling? Their response was to block up the wells. Isaac chose not to quarrel with his neighbours despite their obvious aggression. Instead, he made a decision to move away from them but still remaining in the general area that God had promised him. God came and reaffirmed His promise to Isaac. The scope of God's promised presence and blessings to Isaac related to his remaining in the land allotted to him by God. So, when it appears that there is a famine in your life, be sure of one thing: there will be pain, frustrations, and fear. Sometimes, you may also feel that life is not worth living, but you must stay in the land where God has placed you and rely on His provision. Follow the example of Isaac.

What do you need to do when you stay in the land? You must seek the face of God to find out what and where the problems are. You must also seek revelation for the solution. Many people facing difficulties, say, for example in marriage, refuse to take a reflective approach or ask a crucial question, "Lord, what is the problem?" or "What is causing all this?" or "God, what should I do next?" The man or woman quickly comes to the conclusion that their spouse is the problem. They decide to look for another partner, only to find out that the problem is still there in their new relationship.

I know a man who by all accounts had a terrible first

marriage. The general consensus was that his former wife was the villain. The lead up to the break-up of the marriage and the subsequent divorce battle through the courts reads as one of those modern Hollywood epics. However, as I listened to the story I began to have doubts. Counsellors will be well aware, especially those with experience of mediation in marriage breakdown situations, that when one party sings, their song is so beautiful and sweet that the late Whitney Houston will have to take a back seat. That is, until the other party gives their own rendition.

There are always two sides to a story. It was only as my wife and I began to dig a little deeper, looking at the character of the man, who on the face of it was the wounded party, that we began to realise that he was by no means innocent or guiltless – far from it. What it does show is that we should be slow to draw conclusions, reserving judgment until we have probed and heard the full story from both sides. Unfortunately for the couple, they did not pause, openly and honestly seek solution or submit themselves to appropriate counselling support, before taking up adversarial, win-lose positions. I believe that with the right kind of support, particularly one that challenged the husband regarding his mind-set and attitude, they would have stood a good chance of salvaging their relationship.

Some people in business who have made losses in their ventures often blame bad luck, the next shop on the street, their location, their bank, or business partner. Everyone but themselves. They choose to quit, move into another location or different line of business altogether. As one of my daughters rather pithily said, in a slightly different context, 'It's a bit like cut and paste'. Nothing fundamentally has changed. It is simply a replication of what has gone on before. Very soon they realise that they had not dealt with the underlying issues. The new business suffers the same fate as the previous one; a financial disaster. The key point is that the individuals in these examples failed to make the necessary discovery as to the underlying causes. No discovery, no adjustments, no recovery; but rather a catastrophic replication of disasters.

A rather sobering example is that of the man, Elimelech, who made what on the face of it was the right decision, but which proved ultimately disastrous. We referred briefly to him earlier. His name means 'God is king'. Unfortunately, and with the benefit of hindsight, the kingship of God through His Word was not operative in the life of Elimelech in his decision-making.

Elimelech lived in Bethlehem, in Judah. Bethlehem means the House of Bread. Like Isaac he was confronted by a famine situation. To escape the threat posed to himself and his family by the famine, he took his wife and his two sons, Marlon and Chilion, and travelled to the land of Moab. This was a land of idolatry and all sorts of evil; a land populated by people who were sworn enemies of Israel. Right motive, right intention, but wrong move, wrong place, you might say – and it cost him greatly. In the process of time, Elimelech died and his two sons who had taken Moabite wives also died. Elimelech was left without posterity. He had no male heirs to succeed him and perpetuate his name on earth. The heritage he was seeking to preserve when he chose to leave the place that was under the threat of famine to go down to a seemingly safe place had been wiped out completely.

The grass is not always greener. Be careful where you run to, because what you are looking at may be Astroturf. The lessons are plain for all to see: your survival is not dependent on your ability to choose rationally between alternatives. This is not to condemn Elimelech's decision, but rather to show that in the midst of any recession, economic downturn or indeed any of life's sudden changes and dangerous reversals, you should move only on the basis of what God has spoken to you. God is always speaking but men are not always listening. You only need to listen carefully, discern what He is saying, and obey His voice. That voice could come directly or through the wise counsel of a mature person who has a track record of being able to discern the voice of God and give advice accordingly. It could be loud, soft, progressive or instant. Whatever form it takes, make sure to follow it once you have heard.

What kind of situation are you in right now? Is your spouse threatening to quit the marriage? Are your children in trouble or giving you trouble? Is the area you live in getting worse, and are you worried about the general welfare and education of your children? Do you have a boss who seems to have come straight out of hell? The obvious solution in each of these situations is to move out or move on. Yet we know from Isaac's experience that that often is not God's mind or ideal. He wants you to trust Him to bring you through. His grace and power are most evident in the face of seemingly impossible circumstances.

It is worth noting that it is God who determines when it is right for us not to move or go down to 'Egypt'. Whilst Egypt is a spiritual type for all that is opposed to God, yet throughout the Bible we see how God used individuals, groups and nations that are implacably opposed to Him as instruments to further His purposes. For example, the same Egypt which Isaac was not allowed to go into provided a safe haven for baby Jesus and His parents (Matthew 2:13-15), an event that was prophesied many hundreds of years before it happened (Hosea 11:1). That is the wisdom and power of God at work. What you need to grasp here is that God sets the rules with regard to the 'Egypt' or 'Moab' of each life. Some He permits; others He forbids. The main thing is for you to listen and hear very clearly what God is saying to you before acting. At the crossroads of life, we need to stop and ask God for direction.

Isaac heard clearly from God and obeyed. He chose God's choice. His experience reveals to us the importance of surrendering to God our right to choose. When we do, the blessing that is contained in God's choice comes to us. We need to listen carefully, discern what God is saying and obey His voice. **It is harder to ask God and act on His instruction than to hear from Him.**

I want you to consider some practical application of the truth in the story of Isaac. First, you must realise that there will be conflicts: characterised by satanic attacks, from within and without; and every kind of antagonism, enmity and hostility. Second, you must single-mindedly pursue the promises and blessings given to you, and not get side-tracked by getting into a conflict. Third, you are to remain in the 'frame' of the revelation of God's Word and His promises to you. Fourth, you must realise that God often uses problems and conflicts to shift us out of our comfort zone.

In the process of following a prophetic mandate or pursuing a vision, there will be challenges, at every level. Stay in the land, if you are to recover from any predicament or situation in which you presently find yourself, and prosper in the midst of a challenging environment. Don't drift or run away.

Timeless Truths

- God is always speaking but men are not always listening.

- The challenges that we face today are designed to move us from our comfort zone into a phase and place of greater blessing.

- Many people are languishing spiritually and economically because they have moved from the 'land' which represents the centre of God's will for their lives.

- God often uses problems and conflicts to shift us out of our comfort zone.

- It is harder to ask God and act on His instruction than to hear from Him.

Chapter 5

LEARN FROM HISTORY

'The Lord appeared to Isaac ad said, "Do not go down to Egypt; live in the land where I tell you to live. Abraham obeyed me and did everything I required of him, keeping my commands, my decrees and my instructions." When the men of that place asked him about his wife, he said, "She is my sister," because he was afraid to say, "She is my wife." He thought, "The men of this place might kill me on account of Rebekah, because she is beautiful." ⁸ When Isaac had been there a long time, Abimelek king of the Philistines looked down from a window and saw Isaac caressing his wife Rebekah. So Abimelek summoned Isaac and said, "She is really your wife! Why did you say, 'She is my sister'?" Isaac answered him, "Because I thought I might lose my life on account of her." Then Abimelek said, "What is this you have done to us? One of the men might well have slept with your wife, and you would have brought guilt upon us." So Abimelek gave orders to all the people: "Anyone who harms this man or his wife shall surely be put to death."
(Genesis 26: 2, 5, 7-11)

NYONE reading this book will be aware of the fact that the global economic system has been in the throes of a meltdown since 2008. Here in the United Kingdom, the macro-economic indicators are alarming. A walk through the High Streets of many cities tells its own story. Retail units have closed; major High Street names have either disappeared or are in administration. Business and consumer confidence is at an all-time low and the spectre of further dips in the economy looms large. At a very personal level, many families are deeply affected, and in some families, one or both spouses have lost their jobs. Down-sizing, right-sizing, efficiency drives, restructuring and cut backs are hitting hard at already stressed families. Whatever the terminology, the impact is the same: fear, frustration, and pain.

Today, families are being squeezed on every side by the devastating impact of this global economic downturn. People are hard pressed, and there seems to be no way out of the current mess. Everywhere you turn, people are saying, "We have never seen anything like this before!" Yet, that is not true; you only have to look at the past. Economic recession is nothing new in the world. Many people, whether religious or not, would be aware of the story of the great famine in ancient near East. The Israelites went into a foreign land, Egypt, to look for food, and ended up as slaves for over 400 years. In the New King James version (NKJV) of the Bible alone, the word 'famine' appears no less than 95 times. Ten of these references relate to specific periods in specific geographical locations or areas. Three of such periods relate to three succeeding generations of patriarchs – Abraham, Isaac and Jacob.

Typically, a period of famine is characterised by drought, or lack of rainfall, zero yield from the ground, death of livestock, hunger, disease, and death of human beings through hunger, starvation or disease. The other notable severe famine on record was the one in Samaria, the then northern Kingdom of Israel. The Syrian army had besieged Samaria; nothing could come in or go out. It was so severe that two women agreed to cook their children (2 Kings 6:24 - 7:20).

Fast forward to modern times, *The Great Famine* in Ireland between 1845 and 1851, in which an estimated one million people died, is a major topic in the study of modern economic and social history of Europe. Many died of sickness and hunger. Many lived on the streets and others huddled together in overcrowded work houses. Those who could afford it emigrated as far as Canada, Australia and USA.

Drought and famine were also reported in Asia (India, China, Java, the Philippines and Korea), Brazil, southern Africa, Algeria and Morocco between 1876 and 1879. *The Great Depression* happened before the 'Great Recession' of the 1980s. The last *depression* (a term used to describe when the Gross Domestic Product (GDP) of a country drops by at least 10%) which America suffered was *The Great Depression* in the 1930s and that was preceded by *The Crash* of 1929. The '*Great Depression*' is reputed to be the most severe, most widespread and the longest economic recession of the 20th Century. It started in September 1929 and by the end of October of that year, it had spread around the world, with the stock market crash, affecting both rich and poor.

Another modern form of famine or economic catastrophe

is what has happened on a number of occasions in the Horn of Africa over the last thirty years, with millions of people dead. Our TV screens were filled with horrific images of human suffering at the time.

The question is: "Does the Bible have anything to say on this?" Is there something that will help to guide and support you as you seek to navigate your way through this economic treacherous shoal? God does have something definite to say, and His account is in the Bible. At the time of the very first economic recession recorded in the Bible, we read of God's call to Abram (Genesis 12:1-3), a man who lived in Ur of the Chaldeans, which is generally agreed to be in modern Iraq. God asked him to leave his homeland and embark on a journey of faith. This call was based on an amazing list of promises regarding Abram's future. Responding to the call of God, Abram set out on what turned out to be an incredible journey. When Abram reached the place located between Bethel and Ai, he built an altar and worshipped God (Genesis 12:7-8).

God again appeared to Abram and reaffirmed His earlier promises. Abram built four altars during his earthly walk with God. The altar of vision and revelation was the place where he strengthened his personal relationship with God. The Almighty also revealed Himself and reinforced the promise He had made earlier. As time went on, there was a famine in the land. Abram was caught between the proverbial rock and hard place. Should he stay or should he move? What about the promises of God? What about the well-being of his family? If he stayed, both he and his family were at risk of starvation. The famine was Abram's personal recession and economic meltdown. He had to do something. Staying put, from a rational, perhaps some would say, common sense standpoint, was not an option.

What is the lesson that God is seeking to convey to us here?

The first lesson is that your economic well-being is anchored in God's promises to you, and not on what is happening around you. The promise of blessing to Abram was in relation to the land that he occupied and not in Egypt. In the same way, your provision is in God's Word. God is committed to providing for His children. God's master plan covers every facet of life.

The second lesson is that in the face a recession, you need to hear what God is saying specifically as to what you should do. What may seem to make sense rationally may not necessarily be part of God's will for those who follow Jesus as Saviour and Lord. Abram went down to Egypt when God did not tell him to go. You must therefore be sure that God has spoken to you before you head down to your own 'Egypt' during this economic downturn. You may ask at this point: "What exactly is 'Egypt' and what has it got to do with all this?" 'Egypt' is a spiritual type for all kinds of sin today: idolatry, worship of false gods, oppression, and exploitation. Applying that truth to today, Egypt represents many things; for example, working in an industry that clearly compromises one's Christian faith, all in an effort to put bread on the table.

In my own experience, I can testify how God directed my steps prior to assuming my current role as the National Leader of the UK Apostolic Church. I had for many years worked in business - first in line management roles and then as a management consultant. Throughout my career in business, my decision-making was anchored in what I believed was the call of God on my life, starting with my moving back from the city of Birmingham to the city of London, after my postgraduate studies, to serve and develop in my Christian ministry in the local church where I had come to faith in Jesus. The revelation I had back in 1982 and the ongoing confirmation that came over time acted as a reference point for the decisions that I made.

I remember in the mid-1980s when the UK economy was booming and jobs were plenty. Property prices were going through the roof, not too dissimilar to what happened between 1997 and 2007, in the Tony Blair and Gordon Brown years, when off-plans were being sold and re-sold before the actual structure was completed. The financial wizards and so-called masters of the universe worked their magic, which resulted in toxic debts that brought the global economy and financial systems to its knees. Back in the 1980s, things did not get as bad as they have in more recent times. At that time I worked in marketing management for one of the leading consumer goods companies in the world. People in my field were moving house and changing jobs once every eighteen months. I was tempted to do the same. I felt God say 'No'. This happened on several occasions. At that time it was so frustrating. I could have changed jobs as far back as 1988 or 1989. Each time, I felt what I now know was a prophetic check not to do it. I look back today with gratitude to God for putting me on that leash. Beyond the material, I and my family have not only been blessed spiritually as a result, we have also been spared the massive negative emotional fall-out that invariably results from wrong choices.

What about industries and sectors to work in? This for some, may be controversial, and can be seen to be a matter of personal conscience and choice. I do not drink or smoke. That lifestyle choice, based on my personal reading and understanding of what I believe to be the correct biblical, ethical and moral positions, led me to a decision not to work in either the drinks or the tobacco industry, even though these two sectors paid a premium for marketers. I had many phone calls from recruitment consultants looking for people with my background, qualifications and skills to work for some of the leading players in those two industries. However, my personal conviction meant that I could not take the bait.

I can look back on my experience with the perspective that covers a timescale of three decades. There are three things I would like to mention. First, I am deeply grateful to God for leading me to make the choices that I did. They have helped to make me who I am today. Second, and this is a corollary of the first point, it is that I have no regrets whatsoever. Third, but by no means least, financially, God has blessed me through the years; often through the most unusual ways and means, the testimony of which will be for another book.

The key point was not to go to 'Egypt', either in terms of industry or business sector, driven by desperate economic conditions or personal career ambition. Whilst there are times when God in His infinite wisdom, asks the Josephs (father of Jesus) amongst us to go down to Egypt as a means of protecting His Son from the Herods of this world (as he did with Joseph and Mary in relation to Jesus – Matthew 2:13-15), each of us needs to hear clearly what God wants us to do.

The third lesson is clearly evident: Abram did not first ask God what to do before making his decision. So, the message is that in the midst of recession, you must constantly tune in to God's wavelength, to hear and receive specific revelation, direction and instruction as to what you should do.

I have lived through a number of economic downturns over the years and dealt with three redundancies. As a result I have sometimes said, somewhat tongue in cheek, that I hold a PhD in redundancies. With gratitude to God, my family and I came out of each redundancy financially stronger than we had been before. I had to deal with a redundancy situation in 1996. I joined a company in April 1995 and by July of the same year an announcement was made of a proposed merger between it and another similarly-sized global corporation. The months that followed was characterised by a high level of uncertainty, anxiety, rumours and speculation. Some people jumped ship and moved to other companies when details of the integration plan became public knowledge. I had no such desire. I felt an incredible assurance that all would be well. My boss knew that I was a Christian. I told my boss that I would stay till the very end, make sure that my team of three managers had roles in the new organisation, see what the proposed integration held for me, before making a decision.

I attended all the integration meetings, working with colleagues from the other company to implement the transition plan. Those who have been through such situation will know that people are sometimes tested, but definitely interviewed for job roles that are available, with the most suitable offered a contract in the new organisation. That is how ostensibly it is supposed to work. However, more often than not, so-called mergers end up being the allocation of the spoils of victory by the stronger party. The situation I was in was not too dissimilar. Whilst all this was going on, I got phone call from a recruitment consultant. It was a very attractive opportunity with a well-known company. The remuneration package was significantly higher than what I was on. I smelt a rat. I felt I had been set up by my boss. He was testing to see if I was a man of my word. I explained to the recruitment consultant that I was not interested and that there was a process underway and I would not be making any personal decision to move until I had resettled my team and found out about my own position, because the more senior roles were going to be addressed last.

A day later I saw my boss. I went about my business as usual. He had always respected me in terms of who I was and what I brought to the team and the organisation, but this time his attitude and body language was even more positive. I remember coming home and telling my wife. I had told her about my suspicions about the call from the recruitment consultant. From that time on my boss was even more supportive of me as I went about my business of keeping a focus on running the business whilst transitioning my team.

Two or three weeks later after the call from the head hunter, my boss had found out what was going to happen to me. He called me into his office and told me how deeply unhappy he was that I was not going to be given a role that was equivalent to the one I currently occupied and then promised to give me every support I needed, whatever decision I came to - whether to leave or stay. This was in January 1996. I had been with the company for exactly nine months. By the end of the following month, I was without a job.

Those familiar with employment law will know that what in effect was happening to me was a case of constructive dismissal. The legal position is that in situation where a company is being restructured or merged, employees must be offered equivalent roles in the new organisation; otherwise the company would be deemed to have constructively dismissed them. Once I had made up my mind to leave, my boss swung into action. He gave me huge support about what I would be entitled to by way of a severance package. That sum of money became the sizeable deposit that we used to buy our family home which we still own today.

What are the key lessons? The first is to make sure you hear from God. Once God has spoken and told you to stay, don't go down to 'Egypt', however appealing or attractive it may look. Remain calm, even if others are making a Gardarene rush towards the exit door that leads to 'Egypt'. The second point of application is the need to be a man or woman of your word, even if it costs you. In the end, God will honour you. I look back with a smile on my face as I recall how my boss swung into action to fight my corner and secure the best deal for me; all because I gave my word. He tested me and found it to be true.

Let me say to anyone who is facing a similar situation right now, that it is the job role that has been made redundant, not you. Your skills, experience, know-how and intellect are still intact and relevant. All skills and knowledge are transferable. They may not be needed by your former employers, they are still of use to someone or other organisation. Redundancy relates to role or function in an organisation, not in the person or job holder. The skills, education and training that one has acquired over time do not suddenly desert an individual because their name is removed from the structure or payroll of a company. The skills, most of which are transferable, are still there to be used elsewhere.

The fourth lesson from Abram's experience is that the place called 'Egypt' is a place of compromise, of lies and all kinds of deception. Don't move there unless God says so specifically. When you go down to 'Egypt', you are effectively voting with your feet and moving away from your place of deep and intimate fellowship with God. Abram moved away from the altar which was the centre of his devotional life. The further away he moved from the altar, the place of intimacy with God, the closer he moved towards a life of lies, deception and compromise. This is a lesson you must not fail to grasp.

The fifth lesson is that when you do go down to 'Egypt', you are in effect showing a lack of faith in God and the promise that He has made to you concerning your future. You then move from God's perfect will into God's permissive will. You are not walking by faith but by sight. That is the logical implication of Abram's decision to go down to Egypt. When we go down to 'Egypt' we are moving away from where God has placed us. When we go down to 'Egypt', we are showing a lack of faith in God and the foundational word of promise that He has made to us concerning our future. We move from God's perfect will into His permissive will. We are not walking by faith but by sight.

You need to hear clearly from God before you make a decision to move away from where He has placed you. This applies to all the key areas of our walk with God; touching in particular on family, employment, business, Christian fellowship or service. 'Egypt' represents a spiritual type and moving towards it without a clear word from God leads to all sorts of difficulties. God can help you and wants you to live successfully through any recession. The provision is in His promises. His Word is the cast-iron guarantee for your prosperity. You need to listen and follow what He says. If God has not told you to do so, make sure to avoid today's 'Egypt', in your quest for material well-being and success. If you are in the midst of your own famine, ask God for direction before you take any action; especially the action of walking away from the place of revelation.

Although God graciously prospered Abram whilst he was in the land of Egypt, spiritually he had wandered away from the perfect will of the One who had called him. Don't repeat the mistakes of your forefathers or of the past (Genesis 26:2a). This aspect of God's word to Isaac was very clear: 'Do not go down to Egypt…' (Genesis 26:2a). In other words, Isaac was told to learn the lessons of history and not repeat it or allow history to repeat itself. It was a mistake for Abraham to leave where God had placed him to go down to Egypt (Genesis 12).

Those who forget the lessons of history are bound to repeat it. However, Isaac did repeat one mistake of the past in that he did exactly what Abram his father had done in relation to his wife (Genesis 12:11-13); saying that Rebekah was his sister instead of his wife (Genesis 26:7). Both Isaac and Abram sinned in relation to their wives and in the land of the Philistines. Abram and Isaac lied about the true nature of the relationship of the women they were married to. Both were beautiful women. Fearing for his own safety and wanting to save his neck, Isaac lied in the same way that his father had done. Isaac's deceit was driven by fear for his own well-being. His desperate desire for self-preservation caused him to cruelly expose his wife to all sorts of dangers: rape, adultery, and possibly death (Genesis 26:8-9). Abraham had done the same thing twice in his lifetime. Isaac chose to fear man rather than God. Like father, like son.

One of the saddest features of life is the common pattern of children repeating their parents' mistakes. Non-resident fathers tend to produce children of like bearing. Children of drug and alcohol addicts tend to follow in their parents' footsteps. Greedy or selfish parents tend to produce like children. There is an *Ibo* (one of the major tribes in Nigeria) proverb which says that, 'what is born by a snake will be long'. In Isaac's case, he repeated history, driven by a selfish desire for self-preservation; showing that more often than not, it is easier for children to repeat or reproduce parental weaknesses rather than their strengths. Please note, I said "more often than not." It is not cast in concrete. Children can choose to be better.

Like Isaac, we need to learn from history, and refuse to make the same mistakes of our forebears. This simple truth applies to all citizens of the world. In other words, don't just follow others or follow culture. Re-discover the original blueprint (not the traditions of your forefathers) and follow it. This is even more so for local churches and fellowships. The message is that God can help us and wants to so we can make it through any difficulties and challenges we face, no matter how severe. The provision is in His promises. His Word is the cast-iron guarantee of our prosperity. We need to listen and follow what He says. If God has not told you to do so, make sure to avoid today's 'Egypt' in your quest for modernisation or ministerial success. In the midst of our famine, the task is to ask God for direction; especially if the natural tendency or instinct is to walk away from the place of revelation into a spiritual 'Egypt'.

God is still in the business of revealing His will to those who seek Him earnestly. We are called to be and we must remain a people who walk and move in revelation. By way of specific application, God is saying to the Church to move by revelation and not by impulse, human rationale or the 'everybody is going the same way' line of thinking. We are called to be and we must remain a people of revelation. God is speaking to us: 'Don't go down to Egypt'.

God's word is that we remain planted where He has placed us (stay in your place) and flow in our DNA with an assurance of His presence, blessings and promised inheritance, as we operate in revelation. We are not to leave where He placed us in the spiritual landscape of His will and purposes, unless He specifically tells us to do so.

For all of us, God is saying that we should not deny our identity, either for the sake of convenience, fashion or fear. We should celebrate who we are, rejoice in our uniqueness, and believe that what is in our corporate DNA will be used by God to further the purposes of His kingdom. God is telling us to remain faithful to who we are in Him and what He has called us to be and do.

Timeless Truths

- Those who forget the lessons of history are bound to repeat it.
- Your economic well-being is anchored in God's promises to you and not on what is happening around you.
- You are not walking by faith but by sight when you move from God's perfect will into His permissive will.
- God is still in the business of revealing His will to those who seek Him earnestly.

Chapter 6

FOCUS ON THE KEY ISSUE

*Isaac planted crops in that land and the same year reaped a
hundredfold, because the LORD blessed him. Isaac reopened
the wells that had been dug in the time of his father Abraham,
which the Philistines had stopped up after Abraham died,
and he gave them the same names his father had given
them. Isaac's servants dug in the valley and discovered a well
of fresh water there.   (Genesis 26: 12, 18-19)*

EVERY single day of your life, you will be confronted
with two invitations - an invitation to come up and be
in the will of God for your life, or an invitation to go
down and to align with evil. One invitation will come from
God; the other is from the devil. One will call you up to the
mountain top, to a life of separation, dedication and total
commitment; and getting there can be a tough and lonely
affair. However, the other will call you down to the valley,
where it is green and luscious, like the plains of Sodom and
Gomorrah, which Lot, the nephew of Abraham chose.
Accepting this invitation will delay, damage or destroy your

destiny. Each location has its price, but only one offers a lasting prize.

The other thing you need to realise is that both invitations will come from people; for a deal, a date, extra income, idle chatter, or careless gossip. Whenever you are called to make a decision, ask yourself a number of questions: "Who is this invitation from?" "Will this invitation take me up or drag me down?" "Will this invitation make me or maim me?" "Will it cause me to become distracted from my task and goal, or will it help me to stay on course?"

When the devil invites you to give up your dream, to quit the ministry, to walk away, to pack it all in, to divorce your spouse, or to get involved in ungodly activities, don't forget that the invitation is only an offer. You can refuse it. On the way towards your destiny, there will be many offers, many opportunities, and many invitations to compromise, to take a detour and go down. You have the final say.

Focus is an essential factor when it comes to any form of recovery, whether personal or corporate, moral or social, physical or spiritual. A life that is distracted can never achieve the ultimate; you must stay focused if you are to achieve full recovery. Isaac, the son of Abraham, provides an excellent example of how you can focus and live successfully in the midst of a recession, discovering and re-discovering the resources available to you, and living in super-abundance - materially and spiritually. However, the trouble with humanity and leaders in particular, is that even after they have received and accepted God's word or learned the lessons of history, they begin to drift, forgetting or ignoring the main thing. Here is a well-known saying:

'The main thing is to keep the main thing the main thing.'

Lack of focus or losing sight of the main issue can be caused by a number of factors. Prominent among these is the voice of the people, as happened to King Saul (1st Samuel 13:1-14) and Aaron, the brother of Moses (Exodus 32:1-22). Both suffered severely because they bowed to the pressure of the people. In the New Testament , we have the example of Peter bowing to pressure from those who were determined to drive the infant Church away from the gospel of grace towards legalism. It took the firm and fearless intervention of Apostle Paul to call the drifting Peter back into line with truth (Galatians 2:11-16). Boredom, fickleness, restlessness, impatience, lack of drive, a constant quest for excitement and novelty can all contribute to a loss of focus and the onset of drift. Sometimes people drift because of fear; either for their well-being or in order to maintain their position and status.

Arrogance and rebellion can also lead to drift or a loss of focus away from the main issue, and this is a warning for leaders. I knew a young man some years ago who possessed great potential as a leader. He began well in Christian ministry. However, there was a problem - he was in love with himself. He loved the limelight, the adulation, and the visibility that the leadership stage offered to him. He failed to seek wise counsel or submit himself to other leaders. Not having cut his ministerial teeth properly, or allowed his character to be forged and formed in the crucible of life, he quickly set up his own ministry. Not long after, problems began. The church broke up, his marriage collapsed; he lost his family and his health and never recovered. Sadly, he died some years later. Great potential was wasted because of arrogance and headiness.

There are occasions when it is very clear that the reason why a person has lost focus is that they have been subjected to massive assault by the powers of darkness. The proper response is a counter offensive through spiritual warfare, by the individual and those around him or her. In such situations, you have to engage with the Word of God to realise where your authority lies, confess the word to enforce the will of God on earth, and also deploy the power that flows from a season of intense fasting and prayer.

Isaac refused to drift or become distracted. He maintained his focus on the main thing. Isaac focused on the key issue, which was planting crops and finding water by digging wells. Lack of water meant that new wells had to be dug and old ones re-dug. There is an important point here - in the process of recovery, it is not a case of ancient versus modern or new versus old either, but rather both. Isaac dug new wells and re-dug old ones; the quest was for the same thing - water. Once water is secured, life is sustained. Isaac sowed in the land and reaped a hundredfold. God blessed him and he became prosperous; so prosperous that it provoked jealousy (Genesis 26:12-15).

Isaac began a programme of re-opening some of the wells that his father had dug. He opened the first; the Philistines came and filled it up. He opened the second, and again the Philistines came and blocked it. He moved again and opened the third; this time the wicked Philistines did not come to block it. In response, Isaac declared that God had brought him and his family to a large place, devoid of jealousy, hatred and conflict. That was Isaac's Rehoboth.

The life of Isaac shows to us that in the midst of a recession, we need God to reveal Himself and speak a word of reassurance, instruction and direction to us. You need a word and a clear vision from God. It is this word that will sustain you in the midst of a devastating downturn. Isaac had heard from God, and anchored his life, his choices, and his decision-making on that word. He refused to go down to Egypt; he stayed put. Isaac did not cut a deal with the enemy, or say, 'Guys, we can all share this well;' or say, 'What is mine is yours.' Isaac stayed focused in the face of intimidation; he did not give up. It was his focus and obedience that brought him great blessings.

There are a number of other lessons from Isaac's actions. First, he sowed seed into the ground. That was his main task. In the same way the Church of Jesus Christ must sow the seed of the Word of the gospel of grace, consistently, continuously, and relentlessly. That is the Church's assignment here on earth. Second, Isaac's seed was multiplied and he reaped a hundredfold increase in harvest. The sowing was Isaac's job; God's job was to give increase. Third, Isaac was in the same land as the Philistines. We have no evidence that that they were experiencing the same level of blessing as him.

The Word of God indicates that Isaac was getting water from wells that his father Abraham had previously dug. This shows the need for us to tap into our spiritual DNA. Resources, ancient legacies, bequeathed to us by God through those who have gone before us are waiting for us. Ignorance, pride, a search for new methods, the latest technique, programmes and tools, all lead to the same end – frustration and failure.

Lastly, God's blessing was in Isaac. He carried natural as well as supernatural seed. The Word of God over his life was the supernatural seed, so that anywhere he went in obedience to God's leading, he would prosper. The natural seed which he sowed was a representation of the supernatural seed that was embedded in his life. The blessing of God was not only in his life, but in his hands and in the ancient wells. All that he had to do was to re-open them. I wonder, what ancient wells God is asking you to re-open - as an individual, family, life group, local church, business or movement? I wonder what supernatural seed of God's promises are embedded in your life waiting to be revealed.

The Body of Christ must focus on the key issue - the Church's reason for being - if we are to recover lost ground. Otherwise we are at risk, especially in the Western world, of being distracted by all sorts of side issues and becoming further marginalised and seemingly irrelevant to the wider culture.

The promise of God to bring the Israelites out of Egypt was sure, but as great as that promise was, it required the co-operation and obedience of man. God chose Moses, a very reluctant leader, to go and tell Pharaoh to "Let my people go." The enemy, represented by Pharaoh, was trying to negotiate them out of the promises of God. At various points during the encounter, Pharaoh made no less than four compromise offers to Moses, all in an effort to deflect him from his goal.

Pharaoh's first suggestion was that they should offer their sacrifice in the land of Egypt (Exodus 8:25). Moses refused, saying that they needed to make a journey of three days into the wilderness; to which Pharaoh responded by offering his second compromise. This time it was that the Israelites should not go very far (Exodus 8:28) but Moses stood firm and did not waiver.

Pharaoh's third and fourth offers are worth elaborating upon. He proposed that only the men should leave Egypt; that their women and children be left behind (Exodus 10:10-11). You may ask, 'Of what use is a people without the women, the future mothers, who would birth the next generation; or without the children, the hope of the future?' Leaving Egypt to an unknown destination itself is a risky undertaking; compounded by the fact that the people did not know the route to the place they were going. Moses could have settled for the easier option, to leave Egypt with strong and able men, rather than being saddled with the women and children. However, had Moses settled for the easier option, it would have simply been a matter of time before the men died out - that is if they successfully made the journey - and the nation disappears. But thank God for a leader like Moses who remained focused and refused to be deflected from his main goal; to get every Israelite out of Egypt, with 'not a hoof' left behind.

Pharaoh was not done yet though; he offered a fresh bait - the people could leave Egypt, but without their animals (Exodus 10:24). That seemed like a reasonable offer. But Moses knew that that was not God's perfect will for them. God's ideal for them was total release and recovery; to go away with all that belonged to them. Had Moses and the people accepted that proposal, they would have made a fundamental mistake and at the same time committed a strategic blunder. The animals were what the people of God used to make sacrifices and worship their God (Exodus

10:26). Had they lacked any of those, the atonement of their sins through sacrifices would not have been possible; their worship of God would have suffered, and the predictable consequence of that would have been for them to wallow in sin, lack direction, and ultimately perish in the wilderness. To leave the animals behind also meant that the Israelites would be abandoning significant wealth and their source of food. That was not God's ideal for them. Moses remained uncompromising, totally focused on the main thing.

Attempting to recover a precious item either from the sea or the desert demands great discipline and concentration, while distraction is a big enemy on the road to recovery. Recovering items from the sea can be a hazardous venture, and those with experience in shipwreck salvage missions would attest strongly to this. You may have heard or read about Odyssey Marine Exploration Inc., a company that has been responsible for several high profile shipwreck recovery operations in seas around the world. Odyssey discovered the Civil War-era shipwreck of the SS *Republic* and recovered over 50,000 coins and 14,000 artefacts from the site nearly 1,700 feet deep. In May 2007, Odyssey announced the historic deep-ocean treasure recovery of over 500,000 silver and gold coins, weighing 17 tons, from a Colonial era site code-named "*Black Swan*." In February 2009, Odyssey announced the discovery of Balchin's HMS *Victory*. More recently, Odyssey announced on 18th July 2012 their successful recovery of 48 tonnes (48,000 Kilogrammes) from on board the sunken SS *Gairsoppa*, a 412-foot steel-hulled British cargo ship that sank in February 1941. The haul represents only about 20 per cent of the total treasure on board the sunken merchant ship which was torpedoed by a German U-boat during World War II. The total value of the treasure which lay on the sea bed for over 70 years runs into millions of dollars.

Year after year Odyssey has established itself as major force in the shipwreck salvage industry. But how does Odyssey carry out these expensive and dangerous expeditions? First, they assemble a world-class team of deep-ocean divers, researchers, and equipment. Second, they locate the treasure through sonar and ultra-powered camera technology. Third, they study the elements and the ocean floor; they assess the wreckage and locate the treasure. Fourth, they suck or pull the bounty into their containers. Fifth, they head straight for the market and make some cool money.

If only it was that simple. The truth is that deep-sea divers have to battle with strong under water currents. The people have to penetrate depths in miles, sometimes in territories previously unreached. They have to negotiate dangerous wrecks, ships which sometimes are still loaded with bombs and live ammunition; and they have to work strategically so that there is no loss of cargo or life during each expedition.

You may ask: 'Is it worth all this trouble?' 'Why are these people risking their lives, with no guarantee of success, for treasure that has been lying undisturbed, sometimes for over a century?' The simple answer is that there are lost treasures at sea; there are precious and priceless objects of history that need to be recovered. They have a mission, there is a goal in view and they won't stop until they achieve it. These men are focused, they know what they are after, and are not distracted by the shining sword-fish that no one has seen before, by the red barracudas that follow them on their trail, or by the majestic school of tuna fish in their glorious display. The deep-sea salvage divers are after one thing and one thing only, and that is the recovery of the treasure.

The same is true today for any person, church, or organisation that has to recover lost treasures or past glory. You have to battle the winds and the elements. These are major distractions and obstacles positioned to stop you or to blow you off course. You have to battle the opinion of people that says it is not possible. You have to shun the glitz, the glamour, and the gizmos that have nothing to do with your destiny. You have to battle environments as cold as the icy seas which seek to emasculate your creativity or quench the fire in your belly. If you are to recover, you have to go to great depths that you have never been to before, and come out on the other side with the trophy of recovery and victory in your hands.

The greatest recovery project that history has ever witnessed is the recovery of the sinful man back to God; the salvation of mankind procured through the sinless life, atoning sacrifice and triumphant resurrection of Jesus Christ. The life of Jesus teaches us so much about focus that leads to the place of total recovery. Despite the fact that the birth of Jesus Christ had been prophesised centuries before He was born, the forces of evil, as represented by Herod and his cohorts, wanted to kill Him soon after His birth. Herod tried everything to abort that recovery plan, but baby Jesus' parents escaped with Him and to Egypt.

Jesus had to focus on His assignment; otherwise He would have been deflected from His mission by a long list of distractions and detractors. As a twelve-year-old Jesus went with His parents to Jerusalem to celebrate the feast of Passover, an 80-mile journey from Nazareth, His home town.

At the end of the feast, Jesus' parents were on their way home, only to find out that He was missing. His concerned parents had to turn back to look for Him. Eventually, after a three-day search, they found Him in the temple, listening to, and asking questions of teachers. Mary was obviously relieved, and like any concerned mother would, she asked, "Son, why have you done this to us? Look, your father and I have sought you anxiously" (Luke 2:48, NKJV). You would have thought that Jesus would apologise for His behaviour. He didn't. Rather, He said: "Why did you seek me? Did you not know that I must be about My Father's business?" (Luke 2:49, NKJV). Jesus knew His mission on earth and was resolute in its pursuit, refusing to allow anything to shift His focus. Of course, the obedient boy Jesus later went back home with His parents, who, while recovering from their shock, had to take time to decipher the coded message in their son's response.

Jesus Christ, the God-man who was tasked with the greatest recovery project ever known to mankind, had to wait in the wings to be announced by John the Baptist. Jesus was practically 'on the shelf' for 30 out of the 33 years of His life on earth. When He eventually stepped out on centre stage, He was rejected by the very people He had come to save. The people even said: "Isn't this the carpenters' son?"(Matthew 13:55) But Jesus was secure in the knowledge of His assignment and identity. He maintained His focus.

Distractions also came from different sources and in different forms - accusations, insults, rejection, attempt to make Him a king of the earth, as well as the busyness of life. Jesus did not let the busyness of life, barracking, or the blandishments of men sidetrack Him. He regularly withdrew Himself from the crowd that was thronging Him, in order to spend time alone with the Father.

Jesus did not succumb to the many temptations that He faced. One of such was when Jesus had just finished a 40-day fast. The devil knew He would be hungry, and tempted Him, asking Him to turn stone into bread when he knew Jesus would be at His most vulnerable. Jesus chose to obey His Father rather than submit to the devil. Jesus refused to prove a point; He knew who He was, and was secure in Himself. He refused to bow down to Satan or accept the share of the earthly kingdom with the devil.

Sometimes people think they are acting in your best interest, but are in fact getting in the way. That was what Peter did when he tried to defend Jesus by cutting off the ear of one of the servants that was jeering at Him or by saying he would make sure that Jesus did not go to the Cross. Jesus recognised that it was not Peter speaking but the devil. He said: "Get behind me Satan" (Matthew 16:23). Jesus' ultimate mission was to go to the Cross, and no *help* of man was going to stop Him.

Jesus asked His disciples to pray for Him when the final hour to deliver mankind came, but they all slept off. His betrayal by one of His disciples did not deter Him from the Cross. At a time, Jesus asked the Father if the cup of death could pass over Him, but He nevertheless wanted the will of His Father to be fulfilled. Jesus faced the shame of being unceremoniously hung on the Cross, and that of a slow and agonizing death. Despite His immense power and authority, Jesus refused to come down from the Cross or react impulsively to the people who were mocking, jeering, and insulting Him. Even at that moment, He prayed for their forgiveness.

Jesus faced all these challenges gracefully. If He was not focused or someone with a very clear sense of His purpose, He would have abandoned His mission, come down from the Cross, and dealt ruthlessly with His tormentors, abandoning the work of salvation. Jesus kept His focus on His life's mission – which is to die for the sins of the world.

Timeless Truths

- Lack of focus or losing sight of the main issue can be caused by the voice of the people, arrogance, rebellion, fear and satanic attacks.

- The word of God is what will sustain you in the midst of a devastating downturn.

- Distraction is a big enemy on the road to recovery.

- Sometimes people think they are acting in your best interest, but are in fact getting in the way.

- The greatest recovery project that history has ever witnessed is the recovery of sinful man back to God.

Chapter 7

RECOGNISE, VALUE AND USE WHAT YOU HAVE

Isaac planted crops in that land and the same year reaped a hundredfold, because the LORD blessed him. So all the wells that his father's servants had dug in the time of his father Abraham, the Philistines stopped up, filling them with earth. Isaac reopened the wells that had been dug in the time of his father Abraham, which the Philistines had stopped up after Abraham died, and he gave them the same names his father had given them. (Genesis 26: 12, 15, 18)

You already have what you need for your total recovery. The problem is that for one reason or the other you have not seen or recognised it and therefore have not used it.

2 Kings 4:1-7 is a short narrative of an encounter between Elisha, the prophet, and a widow whose husband had been one of the members of Elisha's school of prophets. This story succinctly illustrates this point about our inability to see what we already have. The widow's problem was that her husband had left her with debts. The creditor was threatening to come and take her two sons as payment for the debt she owed. In

those days, before states and governments created social security systems, children were highly valued for two reasons: first, against enemies who posed a threat to a family's livestock or lands and, second, as a cover for old age. The consequence of the woman's sons being taken away into a life of servitude was that her personal protection and pension plan would be gone forever.

The widow approached and told the prophet her problem. Having listened, Elisha responded with two questions: 'What can I do for you' and, 'What do you have in your house?' She did not answer the first question but went straight to the second: 'I have nothing in the house except a jar of oil.' Elisha told her what to do, which she did. She and her sons went and borrowed containers, cleaned them, poured the small quantity of oil in the jar into the borrowed vessels. The oil kept flowing until they ran out of containers. She went and sold the hugely multiplied oil and used the proceeds to pay off her debts and maintain herself and her sons.

The central point in the story of the widow is that although she was rich, she thought poor, lived poor, and behaved poor. She failed to see what she had. Wealth was in her house but she could not see it. Huge material resources were within her reach, yet she went about empty-handed and poverty stricken. It all had to do with perception, her ability to see. In the jar of oil she saw very little, so she lived as one who had very little. **Her thinking determined her living.** That continued until she met a man who was able to bring out the treasure locked up inside her.

The problem with human beings is that we are always looking over the fence or across the road, at what others have;

and failing to see the wonderful spiritual gifts, talents, abilities and resources that God has given to us. This is a universal truth: what you see drives your thinking and behaviour. Many of us do not value what we have. You need to recognise and value what God has already given to you. We need to look deep inside us and around us, to see what we have already been endowed with. What you need is already inside. Like the widow's oil, it's already in the house. Look carefully and look diligently with a different pair of eyes, and you will spot the gifts, the talents, the resources, and the amazing provision that has always been there.

For many years I carried a prophetic word that one day I would write. In the early 1990s a lady in my local church came up to me and offered to type the manuscript of my book when I came to write it. Two decades later, this book is the first fruit of that prophetic word and personal conviction. She was not the only one; I have had so many prompts, including strong challenges to get on with it and name the date. My response was always that it would be at the right time; God's own time. Yet, at the back of my mind were two things: the lack of time and the apparent lack of research and administrative staff.

When I assumed the role of National Leader of the Apostolic Church, UK, I clearly saw the need to revamp our website, and also to maintain a level of activity that would be of interest to visitors. I wanted to write and post articles. Again, there seemed to be no time. Then it struck me - I remembered a conversation I had with a young lady about ten years before. Walking past during a youth discussion forum, I saw she had a notebook which she would open from time to time to scribble a few things and then close. She did this several times. After the youth forum I called her aside. She must have thought I was going to chide her because of the expression which I saw on her face. On the contrary, I said I had seen her scribbling and could tell she had an interest in writing. I simply encouraged her to keep going.

Ten or so years had passed. She had graduated with a degree in English and American Studies. I mentioned her name to my PA, Mrs Helen Moore, who approached her. She came into the office and I shared the vision I had of writing articles. To cut a long story short, she is now the key resource person for this area of ministry.

Miss Yomi Oladoyinbo is the resource that God had for this ministry. The need and desire brought the revelation. If you pray and look, God will show you the ministry gift or resource person. Now, as and when planned, Yomi would come to the church office with her writing pad, pen and cell phone which functions, amongst other things, as a recording device. I would dictate the articles; she would make notes which would be later transcribed. The materials would come back to me for final editing, prior to publication. Now, lives are being blessed by these articles. The gift had always been there. All I needed to do was to look closely.

Isaac already had all he needed - God's word and revelation. He had the natural seed, plus water from re-dug wells inherited from his father Abraham, in addition to the newly-dug wells. Soil was also in abundance, and so there was enough for Isaac to prosper.

What you already have from God is the key to everything else that you will ever need. If you focus on what you don't have, you will become miserable, repel the spirit of optimism and enthusiasm, and drain the power and energy that flows from a heart of gratitude. Isaac tapped into what was already there. First, he sowed his seed, in the knowledge that he already had the seed of God's word in him. That awareness propelled him to sow the natural seed in the ground. There are many who are carrying prophetic words, true words from God, but who fail to activate and realise it through ignorance, arrogance and indolence. God will not do for you what He expects you to do for yourself.

The story of Elisha and the prophet's widow (2 Kings 4:1-7) that was previously referred to helps to reinforce this point. The woman was in debt and her sons were about to be taken away. She was in a desperate situation. She needed a word of revelation from Elisha before she could see what she had. The instruction of the prophet was followed by her obedience, before multiplication and release from servitude for her two sons could take place. She had to act before the word over her life could be activated. You must do the same.

The widow's story is told by millions of Christians around the world. What is often overlooked by many is that this woman actually had many other things going for her which she did not realise. She had more than the small jar of oil. There were other resources for total recovery that God had placed around her or that she and her late husband had cultivated which needed to be activated in the moment of need. Elisha the prophet asked the widow to go and borrow vessels from her neighbours, and to borrow many.

91

I have had the privilege of living in Africa and in Europe, and of travelling to other parts of the world and seeing how different cultures operate. The principle is more or less the same when it comes to lending out money or other resources. People, banks, and other financial institutions will not knowingly lend to someone who is down to their last penny or drop of oil, or to anyone who is not likely to pay back. The widow was in that category and she had practically nothing. Who would lend her vessels? Who will open the door for her when she came knocking? She was able to do this on two grounds: first, she had the backing of a prophetic word, and second, she probably had good relationships with her neighbours. These points sent her credit rating off the scale.

The relationships that you build over time represent valuable assets for the future. I am not referring to modern-day networking that is driven by selfish motives and a desire to use, and in some cases, abuse others for profit. The message is that you should invest in relationships. The good relationship that the widow had with her neighbours was probably the result of long-term nurturing on her part and possibly that of her late husband. Between them they had built powerful relational bridges with those around them. In the same way, we all must build good relationships. Serve others, serve humbly and sacrificially; give of yourself, your time, and your resources, without expecting anything in return.

In Acts 10:1-48 we read the story of a man called Cornelius, a centurion, who lived in first-century Caesarea, a city in the ancient Near East. His life was hallmarked by his devotion to God and his amazing generosity. He prayed to God always and gave alms. Cornelius was extremely charitable. One day, an angel of God appeared to him and said, 'Your prayers and your charitable deeds have come up for a memorial before God.' What this tells us is that our devotion to God and our generosity to man act as credit deposits in heaven. One day heaven will respond to us, with a huge return on our investment. Give yourself in serving others. One day, in your hour of need, God will activate the storehouse from above, using unusual and unexpected sources to bless and bring you to the place of total recovery.

There are some further insights to be gleaned from the story of the widow. We have already established that for her to have been able to borrow from her neighbours in the condition she was in at that time meant that she had, at least in the past, been a good neighbour. She was someone who was not quarrelsome, and who had probably returned items borrowed in the past; a woman with a good character, whose word could be trusted. She was not like some people today, who when you lend them an item or money you may have to resort to a recovery service, debt collector or the courts, in order to secure the return of your money or goods. Not the widow. She called upon and leveraged the reputation she had developed over time, and when she needed to borrow vessels people were willing to lend to her.

A further point is the fact that this woman possessed instinctive marketing and business skills, which until that time had not been given the opportunity to emerge and flourish. Just imagine, a woman whose husband had died, a widow who had nothing and was living on the edge of poverty; someone who was contemplating what would happen after her two sons had been taken into bonded labour, and who suddenly found herself on the streets in the marketplace as an oil dealer. That is some transformation. Remember, the prophet told her, 'Go sell the oil, pay off your debt, and live on the rest.' The prophet did not say, 'Great; load the oil in my truck, I will go and sell it for you, and transfer the money into your account.' He said in effect, 'Go and sell for yourself, and transact in what you now have. Run your own business. Do your own deals. You make the profits.' There is no record in the Bible that the woman had a degree in Economics or went to a business school. For you or anyone to sell and make a profit, you will need to be able to produce, package, promote, and price your goods, as well as being able to persuade people to buy from you. She must have been good with people and possessed good sales and customer management skills. In today's world, she would have been someone who is able to prepare invoices, issue receipts, and keep records of her outgoings and income. Otherwise she wouldn't have been able to separate the capital from the profit.

The world of business is full of examples of what it means to use what you have. Many years ago, Kellogg's launched its Kellogg's Crunchy Nut Flakes line. The story goes that when the company was looking for business growth opportunities, it looked within and outside its four walls. In the end it chose to leverage assets that it already had. Not only did they have a strong brand name in the Kellogg's name, they had a strong brand that had virtually become generic for the category, as well as being synonymous with breakfast. The third asset was their know-how in cereal technology, especially turning corn into cornflakes. Combining a number of their internal assets together – namely technology, a strong brand heritage and marketing know-how - they launched Crunchy Nut flakes. They used clever marketing to position the line as new and different, when all it is cornflakes coated with honey, sugar and nuts. Over the years the product has generated billions of pounds for Kellogg's, spawned a number of imitators, but is still going strong. Kellogg's used what they already had. How about you? What do you have? Use it.

Those from an older generation in the UK will remember the heyday of Burton's menswear. Burton's was the leading men's suit retailer in the UK. However, in the late 1960s and 1970s, competition was rife, shopper habits were changing, whilst Burton's business model was not able to cope. The supply chain was a mess, costs were spiralling out of control, merchandise was out of step with what consumers were looking for and the stores were dated, with a workforce that was increasingly caught in a time warp. The first attempt at transformation and recovery was the appointment by the Board of Directors of a new CEO, a man with an MBA from one of the leading business schools at the time. He hired managers after his own image. Whilst the CEO and his team were no doubt highly competent individuals, the problem was that they did not fully understand the key business issues facing the company, especially underlying cultural issues in the business. He and his team failed to turn the business round and were duly relieved of their duties. He was replaced by an insider, a young man barely in his forties by the name of Ralph Halpern. The rest, as they say, is history.

Over a number of years Halpern (later knighted by the Queen) transformed the business into one of the leading names on the High Street, as well as founding Top Shop, another major clothing retailer in the UK.

Instead of blaming the devil when your business is not moving as fast as expected, go back to the basics; discover what the problems are, determine to fix them, use the resources already available to you, and recover from your economic downturn. You might not have a job today, but you still have something inside you. Your skills are still there. It is the old job role that is redundant, not you. The vast majority of skills, especially people skills, are transferable. It might be your skill in selling, in sowing, or in setting up. Reach deep inside you today, discover what you have, and use it. It may also be skills that others around you have. They are God's gift to you. If you have invested in other people in the past, be bold and ask for help. You will be surprised at the response.

You have to use what God has given you to get to where you are going. I remember reading a newspaper article on Jon Favreau, the speech writer described by President Barack Obama as his "mind reader", and one of the youngest chief presidential speech writers in recent history. Favreau was a man credited for many of the great speeches made by the President, and he had worked with Obama since 2004, when he was first noticed by the then Senator, now President.

What exactly happened? Jon Favreau's career took off when, at age 23, he interrupted U.S. Senate candidate Barack Obama during a speech rehearsal to offer some suggestions for improvement. At the time, Favreau was working as a junior speech writer for Senator John Kerry who was at the time the Democratic Presidential candidate nominee. John Kerry's staff had noticed an overlap between Obama's speech and the one John Kerry had planned to deliver. The speech to be delivered by a senatorial candidate must not upstage that of a presidential candidate at the party's convention. Favreau was the one sent to ask Obama to trim his text. Of all people at the disposal of the national Democratic Party at the time, sending Favreau, a 23-year-old junior speech writer to do the task was not only mean but cruel. But ... Favreau did the job!

After Obama was elected to the U.S. Senate, he hired Favreau, who later joined him on the 2008 Presidential election campaign. The rest is history. Obama won the presidential elections and Favreau went to work in the White House as the director of speech writing in Obama's first term as President. Favreau has now bowed out as chief speech writer after a four-year stint at the White House. Favreau was not a legislator and did not have the legal and the political acumen of the men he was dealing with but he used the skill that God endowed him with.

Many people have hidden skills, talents, and abilities; relationships, connections and networks. The same is true for communities and nations. They are all of God's means of taking us to the place of total recovery. In Isaac's case, he had seed, he had wells, he had servants, and above all, he had the promises of God. He used all of them. What do you have today? Unless you ask this critical question and use what you have, your God-endowed assets will lie idle and your recovery will be a long way off.

Sadly, the vast potential that many people possess has been left idle and unused. No country in Africa or Asia or other part of the developing world has been able to get out of poverty through Western aid or hand-outs. The same is true for individuals. Carlos Slim, the richest man in Mexico, who in 2010 was on the Forbes list as the richest man in the world (and still is, today), was quoted in the Wall Street Journal in October 2010 as saying that "charity doesn't solve anything" and achieves little. These were his exact words: "The only way to fight poverty is with employment. Trillions of dollars have been given to charity in the last 50 years, and they don't solve anything." Mr Slim, a controversial figure who has been involved in charitable projects with the Bill and Melinda Gates Foundation was pointing the world to an obvious fact that the best way to fight poverty is to create jobs and to stimulate productivity. Let people be given the opportunity to use what they already have – their energy, creativity, desire, skills and God-given abilities, and then things will change.

Several countries in the developing world are endowed with tremendous natural resources – fertile lands, vast expanse of savannah, petroleum oil, beautiful topography capable of generating hydroelectric or wind power, and an array of mineral resources. Some of these countries don't realise what they have, or cannot tap into them. These nations refuse to discover and so cannot recover from their present economic woes. Instead of digging deep into themselves, they choose to look elsewhere, and at other people and other countries for succour or aid. Despite assistance from the outside world, many remain in terrible conditions.

If you have ever been to Italy, or visited or lived in any of the major cities in the world where good coffee is served, you will not fail to notice the fuss made about Italian coffee in its various forms. You can order an espresso, doppio, ristretto, lungo, macchiato, corretto, cappuccinos (scuro, chiaro), a latte or latte macchiato. Along with opera, fashion, and cars, it is hard to think of Italy without coffee. According to a website promoting Italian life, "Without Italy, Starbucks would not exist and without coffee, Italy would grind to a halt." I will leave to you to judge whether that claim is true.

Coffee drinking in Italy is part of the national culture, part of the modern lifestyle in the West, and a mega-billion dollar industry around the world. However, coffee did not originate from Italy but from the highlands of Ethiopia in Africa. Coffee did not even reach Europe for thousands of years. Most of the coffee drunk in the world today comes from South America and Indonesia, not Italy. However, what the Italians have perfected is the art of choosing good coffee beans, the art of roasting, blending, brewing, selling and serving coffee in its various forms. The Italians, and to a lesser extent, the French, have also perfected the art of marketing the desirability of drinking coffee in bars and cafés, or making it at home with elegant coffee-making machines. Italians don't have coffee grown in their backyard but they have used the knowledge and skill they have to create a culinary culture that has found near-global acceptance.

Year after year, millions of dollars are spent to clear seaweed from waterways in areas of Nigeria, and in other countries on the grounds that it impedes marine transport. According to governments and their agencies, the clearing of these waterways benefits the communities in these areas, as it makes it easier for the flow of goods and services, and allows connection with other parts of the world. The government agencies saddled with this responsibility argue passionately that clearing seaweeds is ultimately, for economic growth. What is particularly concerning about many of these countries where the seaweeds and hyacinth are seen as a scourge is that research and several studies have been conducted which suggest the many potential good uses of these seaweeds. For example, apart from producing a rich living environment for fish and other vertebrates, seaweeds are rich in soda and potash, which can be used in the industrial manufacture of soaps, glass, and iodine, as well as being excellent sources of vitamins, amino acids, carbohydrates, proteins, lipids, and growth hormones. Many seaweed species are also used as food throughout Asia and the Pacific region.

You may have heard this before: 'One man's food is another man's poison.' That can be very true. While some regions of the world are moaning about the presence and problem (as they see it) of seaweeds along coastal waters and pathways, other countries are aggressively cultivating seaweed for chemicals, drugs, food and fuel. I recently read about the extensive cultivation of seaweeds in China, aimed at the production of food, textiles, cosmetics, printing and medicine. Now researchers are developing ways to turn the sugars and starches seaweeds contain into cost-effective biofuel to replace conventional diesel and petrol from fossil fuels and green fuel made from land crops. Nigeria, which has a main coastline of about 860 km and a coastal zone which has the largest area of mangroves on the African continent, yet continues to have limited information on her seaweed resources, or their biomass, which could be used for the various purposes that have been mentioned.

Just in case it has been lost in the many examples, the message is this: as individuals or groups, peoples or nations, God has given us all that we need for total recovery. All we need to do is to recognise and deploy them. What is it that has God given to you, to me, and to us? We need to (re)discover all of these in order to recover. Let us apply ourselves in using them, and as we do, we will surely prosper.

Timeless Truths

- What you already have from God is the key to everything else that you will ever need.

- If you focus on what you don't have, you will become miserable, repel the spirit of optimism and enthusiasm, and drain the power and energy that flow from a heart filled with gratitude.

- What you see drives your thinking and behaviour.

- Give yourself in serving others. One day, in your hour of need, God will activate the storehouse from above, using unusual and unexpected sources to bless and bring you to the place of total recovery.

Chapter 8

THE BLUEPRINT OF GOD

The Lord appeared to Isaac and said, "Do not go down to Egypt; live in the land where I tell you to live. Stay in this land for a while, and I will be with you and will bless you. For to you and your descendants I will give all these lands and will confirm the oath I swore to your father Abraham. I will make your descendants as numerous as the stars in the sky and will give them all these lands, and through your offspring all nations on earth will be blessed, because Abraham obeyed me and did everything I required of him, keeping my commands, my decrees and my instructions." So Isaac stayed in Gerar. Isaac planted crops in that land and the same year reaped a hundredfold, because the Lord blessed him. Isaac reopened the wells that had been dug in the time of his father Abraham, which the Philistines had stopped up after Abraham died, and he gave them the same names his father had given them. Isaac's servants dug in the valley and discovered a well of fresh water there. Isaac built an altar there and called on the name of the Lord. There he pitched his tent, and there his servants dug a well. (Genesis 26:2-6, 12, 18-19, 25)

THE world we live in is built on principles and values. These are foundational. They are there by design, put in place by God the Creator of the universe. We function best and prosper most when we operate within the moral and spiritual framework that God has established. This is true of the individual as it is of people-groups and nations. These principles and values together constitute what I have chosen to call God's blueprint for living. They were there at the dawn of creation. They were the basis of God's relationship with Adam and Eve, and framed the relationship that God established between Himself and the children of Israel. Following them brought blessings, progress, and prosperity; violation however brought the exact opposite –curses, regression and poverty.

It begs the question: what is a blueprint? What is it all about? The exact definition of a blueprint may be slightly different depending on the area of life you are addressing, but the same theme runs through almost all the meanings. Having its roots in drawing and architectural designs, a blueprint is a reproduction of a technical drawing, documenting or engineering design, using a contact print process on light-sensitive sheets. This was the original process. It allowed rapid and accurate reproduction of documents used in construction and industry by using light coloured lines on a blue background, a negative of the original. Essentially when the tracing is made exactly according to the blueprint, you get exactly the same pattern as the original. So the secret and the power are in the fidelity – or staying true to the dictates of the pattern of the blueprint. If you deviate from the pattern of a blueprint, you will not achieve the same results as the original.

How then does this definition apply in Isaac's case and to you? You will get a better understanding by looking at aspects of God's blueprint to Isaac regarding his future.

Scope

Scope refers to the area or space for movement, operation or activity that a person or corporate body has. It sets out the extent, range or limit of what that individual or group can legitimately do. It is defines the mandate that has been given. It is essentially a legal concept in that is often seen in the area of constitutional or administrative law. When a governmental or non-governmental agency does anything outside what it has been permitted to do in law, such acts are deemed to be, using a Latin expression, *ultra vires*. In other words, the agency has acted beyond its powers. Such infractions will attract a penalty. In the Bible, this was first seen in relation to Adam and Eve. God had placed them in the Garden of Eden and given them a very clear set of instructions. This defined the expected scope of their behaviour. Adam and Eve however stepped outside the bounds set for them by God. Their disobedience led to judgment, banishment and separation from God's presence. Humanity is still suffering as a consequence.

Another example of a defined scope is in relation to Joshua. Moses who had led Israel for forty years and through the wilderness to the very edge of the Promised Land had died. The mantle of leadership was now in the hands of Joshua. God spoke the following words to Joshua:

"Moses my servant is dead. Now then, you and all these people, get ready to cross the Jordan River into

the land I am about to give to them — to the Israelites. I will give you every place where you set your foot, as I promised Moses. Your territory will extend from the desert to Lebanon, and from the great river, the Euphrates — all the Hittite country — to the Mediterranean Sea in the west. No one will be able to stand against you all the days of your life. As I was with Moses, so I will be with you; I will never leave you nor forsake you. Be strong and courageous, because you will lead these people to inherit the land I swore to their ancestors to give them. "Be strong and very courageous. Be careful to obey all the law my servant Moses gave you; do not turn from it to the right or to the left, that you may be successful wherever you go. Keep this Book of the Law always on your lips; meditate on it day and night, so that you may be careful to do everything written in it. Then you will be prosperous and successful. Have I not commanded you? Be strong and courageous. Do not be afraid; do not be discouraged, for the LORD your God will be with you wherever you go." (Joshua 1:2-9)

The promise to Joshua relates to a defined territory - from the desert of Lebanon to the Euphrates, the Hittite country, and the Mediterranean Sea in the west. The promise is backed by two specific commands: first, to be strong, bold and courageous; second, to meditate and fully obey the Lord's commands. God also promised His abiding presence. The physical or geographic scope of God's blueprint to Joshua was clearly defined. He was commanded to remain within its terms. If he failed to obey God, or go looking for territory that was not promised to him, he could not expect the Lord's continued presence or protection. Neither could he reasonably expect prosperity or success.

Scope therefore is a boundary. It is the limits of the architectural drawing. In Isaac's case, God told him to live in the land. He was promised God's presence, as well as his future inheritance of the land; re-affirming the original covenant that God had made with his father Abraham.

There is a universal blueprint that God has drawn that defines His relationship with mankind. This blueprint is set out in His word, the Bible. However, there is a blueprint for each one of our lives. It defines the mandate that the Maker has given to each one of us. That blueprint is activated the moment we accept Jesus as our Saviour and Lord. The task that we have is to discover and walk in it every day.

Promise, Position and Place

The blueprint that Isaac was given by God consisted first of an instruction to stay in the land. He was to remain there for some time. The second is a promise of an inheritance. God gave a promise that not only placed Isaac in a given location but positioned him for the future. In the same way the blueprint that God has for your life consists of a set of promises linked to an instruction. The combined effect of the promises and instructions places you within the scope of His eternal purpose and positions you for a blessed and prosperous future. The key that triggers the fulfilment of God's promises is your obedience.

Potential, Power and Prosperity

Every blueprint has embedded within it the capacity for success. It is a carrier of the potential for successful replication. The words that God spoke to Isaac were imbued with potential but it also had power. According to the Bible, there is power in God's Word:

> *As the rain and the snow come down from heaven, and do not return to it without watering the earth and making it bud and flourish, so that it yields seed for the sower and bread for the eater, so is my word that goes out from my mouth: It will not return to me empty, but will accomplish what I desire and achieve the purpose for which I sent it.*
> *(Isaiah 55:10-11)*

God's word is supreme.

> *Since a king's word is supreme, who can say to him, "What are you doing?" (Ecclesiastes 8:4)*

All that is required for progress, blessing and prosperity is to follow the blueprint of God. Jesus' earthly ministry was based on a blueprint from His Father, which He duly followed.

> *He went to Nazareth, where he had been brought up, and on the Sabbath day he went into the synagogue, as was his custom. He stood up to read, and the scroll of the prophet Isaiah was handed to him. Unrolling it, he found the place where it is written: 'The Spirit of the Lord is on me, because he has anointed me to proclaim good news to the poor. He has sent me to proclaim freedom for the prisoners and recovery of sight for the*

blind, to set the oppressed free, to proclaim the year
of the Lord's favour.'
(Luke 4:16 -19)

The purpose of the Church is to fulfil the blueprint that Jesus has set out.

Therefore go and make disciples of all nations, baptizing them in the name of the Father and of the Son and of the Holy Spirit, and teaching them to obey everything I have commanded you. And surely I am with you always, to the very end of the age."
(Matthew 28:19-20)

But you will receive power when the Holy Spirit comes on you; and you will be my witnesses in Jerusalem, and in all Judea and Samaria, and to the ends of the earth." (Acts 1:8)

That blueprint will be fulfilled because it is God's greatest passion.

Of the greatness of his government and peace there will be no end. He will reign on David's throne and over his kingdom, establishing and upholding it with justice and righteousness from that time on and forever. The zeal of the LORD Almighty will accomplish this. (Isaiah 9:7)

At the heart of the problems faced by mankind today is our desire to do what pleases us rather than that which delights the heart of God. Adam and Eve deviated from the blueprint and sinned against God by eating of the fruit of the tree of the knowledge of good and evil in the Garden of Eden. This was an act that led to man's separation from God. This reality is re-enacted billions of times each day as human beings make choices and decisions that run contrary to the will of the God who created them. He is the God who has revealed Himself in the person of His Son Jesus. He is a God of principles and patterns. He works out His agenda according to His Will. The will of God in every situation is for man to follow His blueprint. For those who love and serve Him, God has said in His Word:

For I know the plans I have for you," declares the LORD, "plans to prosper you and not to harm you, plans to give you hope and a future. (Jeremiah 29:11).

God's blueprint applies in every situation of life. The life of Israel as a nation in the Old Testament period is characterised by a cycle of rebellion against God, punishment and attendant suffering, followed by repentance and restoration. Repentance and return is what is required where we have violated the blueprint either through ignorance, indifference or deliberate choice.

In the story recorded in 2 Kings 23:1-25, the people of Israel had been in one of those spiritual and moral mess phases. Josiah had been crowned king at the very tender age of eight years. In the eighteenth year of his reign, he gave orders for the payment of those who worked in the maintenance and general upkeep of the temple. In the course of that assignment the high priest found the book of the law which was read to the king's secretary, who in turn brought it to the king. Josiah was grieved when he found out the gap between how they lived as a people and the requirements of the book of the law and the judgment that the nation faced as a consequence.

King Josiah humbled himself, showing this by the symbolic tearing of his robes and crying out to God for mercy. Then he began one of the greatest acts of reformation ever recorded in the Bible. The king took steps to discover what the divine blueprint for the nation was, and then took consistent, concrete measures towards recovery. Repentance was the key. This was followed by reformation, evidenced by the destruction of every vestige of idolatry, renewal of worship and devotion to God, plus a change in the structures that underpinned how society operated. The law of God was brought centre stage. It informed their thinking and action. Such was his leadership in his acts of seeking to bring the nation back to God's original blueprint, that this was said of him:

Neither before nor after Josiah was there a king like him who turned to the LORD as he did—with all his heart and with all his soul and with all his strength, in accordance with all the Law of Moses. (2 Kings 23:25).

What do you need to do in order to recover the original blueprint? The same is true in any recovery, whether you are dealing with recovery of materials or dealing with individual lives, families, marriages, businesses, organisation or automobiles. An example of what happens when a car breaks down on the road may not be universal but it is a common feature of life in developed countries. In the UK major service providers include firms such as the AA, RAC, and Green Flag. The model is that you pay a fee, either monthly or annually, for an agreed service package. This payment commits the recovery service provider to come and find you and your vehicle should you break down or find yourself stranded in the middle of nowhere.

When a car breaks down, it means that something has temporarily rendered the vehicle unfit for purpose. A car is meant to run from A to B. Failure to do so is a departure from purpose or the manufacturer's blueprint. When your car has broken down on the road, and you have a recovery service contract with the AA or RAC, the first thing you have to do is to make a telephone call to the service provider and ask for assistance. First of all, you must have a valid contract with the service provider; otherwise they are not legally obliged to attend to you and your vehicle. In the same way, you have to call on God if you really want to be rescued. Applying the idea of a contract, your relationship with God through faith in His Son Jesus secures you the right to call on Him. God in His infinite mercy looks at the heart to see if there is humility, contrition and a deep desperation that places all on God.

God clearly invites you to call Him. The Bible is filled with this message:

Call upon Me in the day of trouble; I will deliver you, and you shall glorify Me. (Psalms 50:15, NKJV).

Seek the LORD while he may be found; call on him while he is near. Let the wicked forsake their ways and the unrighteous their thoughts. Let them turn to the LORD, and he will have mercy on them, and to our God, for he will freely pardon. (Isaiah 55:6-7).

Call to Me, and I will answer you, and show you great and mighty things, which you do not know. (Jeremiah 33:3, NKJV)

The next thing that will happen once you call the automobile recovery service is for them to ask you a few questions to find out what exactly has happened. You will hear from the operator at the other end of the line asking: "Where are you?" or "What is the problem?"

Incidentally, that was the same question that God asked Adam after he and Eve had sinned. They tried to hide themselves from God. The Lord asked a simple question: 'Adam, where are you?' and 'What is this you have done?' 'Where are you?' is a fundamental question that must be asked if you are to ever have a chance of recovering from a difficult situation. And for the recovery of an automobile that broke down, this is perhaps the most important question that you will have to answer.

If you have been sensible enough to let the recovery engineer know where you are, they will ask you to wait for them. Most people in their right mind would know that they have no option other than to wait for the recovery man, the person who has the ability to recover them and their vehicle. Growing impatient, going back into the car, trying to start engine, or throwing tantrums will not lead to recovery. However, people do ridiculous things every day. Rather than wait for God the master rescuer, they burn themselves out in a vain attempt to bring about the desired outcome. Some even try to *fake* it in order to *make* it. But the key is to call on God, wait for Him, the only one who can rescue you. Only He can fix the vehicle. He knows how the car operates. In fact, He knows exactly where the damage is and what has caused it. Allow Him to take charge of the vehicle of your life and He will fix it using His blueprint.

Timeless Truths

- Every blueprint has embedded within it the capacity for success.

- A blueprint is a carrier of the potential for successful replication.

- God's blueprint applies in every situation of life.

Chapter 9

WALK IN OBEDIENCE

*So Isaac stayed in Gerar. Isaac planted crops in that land
and the same year reaped a hundredfold, because the LORD
blessed him. Isaac reopened the wells that had been dug in the
time of his father Abraham, which the Philistines had
stopped up after Abraham died, and he gave them the same
names his father had given them. Isaac's servants dug in the
valley and discovered a well of fresh water there. But the
herders of Gerar quarreled with those of Isaac and said, "The
water is ours!" So he named the well Esek, because they
disputed with him. Then they dug another well, but they
quarreled over that one also; so he named it Sitnah. He
moved on from there and dug another well, and no one
quarreled over it. He named it Rehoboth, saying, "Now the
LORD has given us room and we will flourish in the land."
(Genesis 26:6, 12, 18-22)*

OBEDIENCE to God's Word is the bedrock of total
recovery and prosperity. There is no solution outside the framework of what God has revealed in His
Word. Following God's principles is the pathway to experiencing His presence and provision. Isaac was obedient and

God blessed him with great wealth. Even though there was famine in the land, Isaac did so well that he was said to be very prosperous.

Obedience demands that you follow the blueprint that God has given to you, regardless of what others think. The tendency is to eschew the rigour and discipline inherent in following the God-given agenda in favour of seemingly easier options, or what you are comfortable doing, or what you are used to. Digging is hard work. Farming is hard work. Hostility is a pain. Yet, you must persist in obedience because God has spoken. The God who spoke will enable you to attain your goal. Your obedience to God's Word, allied to the hard work of digging for water, the soil and sowing seeds, is what will produce the promised blessing.

The centrality of God's Word as the source of your provision and preservation in these recessionary times cannot be underestimated. A constant refrain throughout this book is that our security lies in what God has said, not what we think or what the economists, politicians, analysts or other experts have said. Your security is made a reality by your obedience. It follows that if you do not obey, you cannot experience the miracle of supernatural, super-abundant, unceasing supply.

Isaac was in the same land as the Philistines. There is no evidence they were experiencing the same level of blessing. Isaac drew water from wells that his father Abraham had previously dug. The blessing was in the man by virtue of the word he had received, his seed and the water from the old wells. As long as he walked in obedience to the word of God to him, the blessings flowed and overflowed. Everything that Isaac did was contrary to common sense. When there is famine (lack of finance, personal progress, numerical or financial growth), you want to move away. When there is conflict, hostility or other forms of negative attitude, you want to run away. When there is naked aggression, you want to get back, fight fire with fire, with no quarters given and no prisoners taken. Isaac did none of that. He simply obeyed God, stayed and sowed in the land, and prospered.

The Bible is full of accounts of obedience in the face of seemingly impossible situations. The account in 1 Kings 17:1-24 opens in dramatic fashion, with Elijah prophetically declaring a famine over the land, which was to last for many years. God first directed him to a brook called Kerith, where he would be miraculously fed by a raven, an unusual, divinely-ordained courier service. In the process of time, the brook dried up and the raven-led supply chain was shut down. Elijah was told to go to a foreign land, a place called Zarephath in Sidon (modern day Lebanon). The word of God was the basis of the prophet's removal from the brook Kerith to Zarephath. God spoke, Elijah the prophet obeyed.

Even more astonishing is the fact that Elijah was directed to a widow who had nothing. On arrival there, Elijah met the widow, who had an only son. She was on her way to gather sticks for fire wood, to cook her last meal for herself and her son to eat, and await inevitable death. Elijah asked her for a cup of cold water. As she was on her way to fetch the water, Elijah asked her to prepare a meal for him. She explained her situation; that all she had was a very small quantity of flour and an equally small amount of oil, with which she was going to prepare a meal for her and her son, and then await death. Elijah asked her to prepare something for him first, and then made an amazing prophetic pronouncement concerning the little quantity of oil and flour that she had left. She obeyed the prophet's word, prepared a meal for him, before cooking the one for herself and her son. Again, God's word through Elijah concerning the small quantity of oil and flour that the widow had was the basis of her confident repose. The result was that they had a continuous supply of food until the famine or recession of their day was over.

Unfortunately, death struck. The son of the widow became ill and died suddenly. That was a devastating tragedy that had serious implications for the widow's economic and social position. In those days, as in many cultures around the world today, sons were greatly valued, for many reasons. They were considered to be the protectors and providers for their parents in old age, particularly their mothers, who could be exploited and abused by unscrupulous relatives of their husband if there were no sons. Sons in essence were the personal protection and pension plan of their parents. This widow was no exception. Death it seemed had robbed her of both. In response, Elijah prayed to God and the son came back to life. So, not only did the woman experience the miracle of divine provision of food, she also experienced a miraculous restoration of her son back to life. Her obedience was the key to her preservation and the restoration and recovery of her dead son.

Obedience is like a seed that is sown in God. That seed is secure forever. What is sown in God cannot and will not die. It may seem to die, but God will bring it back to life. When you put God first, He will take care of you. Through her obedience, by first giving food to Elijah, the woman had sown and by faith secured her life and that of her son in God. Her action was a demonstration of great faith in the prophetic word from a stranger and a foreigner that she had never met before. Her life and that of her son were hidden in God because of her obedience. Death could not take her son away. God will do the same and more for you, only if you can obey Him.

There is another miraculous story of recovery and restoration in the life of another woman from a place called Shunem (2 Kings 4:8-37; 8:1-6). The parallels of her story with that of the widow of Zarephath are simply amazing. This time the central character is the prophet Elisha, Elijah's servant and successor. The woman had shown incredible kindness to Elisha, providing food and shelter for him and his servant, Gehazi, during their journeys. Elisha and Gehazi would lodge in the woman's house each time they travelled. Seeing their need for a place to stay, the woman and her husband built a room in their house specifically for the prophet and his servant. God rewarded her selfless giving. Her reward was the unprompted prophetic promise of a son, who was duly born. However, in the process of time the child died. Like Elijah before him had done, God used Elisha to raise the Shunamite's son.

Later, as famine (recession) threatened the land, Elisha told the Shunamite woman to go with her family to another country until the famine was over. She went away for seven years while the famine raged. When she returned, she found that her property had been illegally seized. Just as she made her way to present her appeal to the king for the return of her assets, Gehazi, Elisha's servant was telling the king the story of what God had done through Elisha in the woman's life. The central character of his narrative was right before the king. Having presented her case, the king ordered the return of all her property, plus accrued interest. Incredible! That's how God works in the lives that have sown in obedience to His will.

There are many lessons from the story of the woman from Shunem and the widow of Zarephath. First, your generosity and sacrifice in service to God will be rewarded. It is an investment that will always yield a return, in normal times as well as during economic downturns. Second, what God gives to you, He will restore back to life, even if it seems to have died. Third, there are times in the course of a recession when God will direct you to an economic haven, in order to preserve you and your family; as he did when he asked Elijah to go to the brook Kerith, and the woman from Shunem to leave for a foreign land. Elijah obeyed and was provided for; the woman obeyed and was preserved. Last but by no means least, is the restoration of the woman's assets, with interest, which is evidence that God is able to restore to His children, post-recession, every asset secured in Him which has been wrongly taken away. Somebody, somewhere, somehow, will speak on behalf God's children, as Gehazi did on behalf of the woman.

Many in life are great achievers academically and socially in different fields of human endeavour. Yet there is a key area in need of recovery. The single biggest area of recovery for mankind is to know the forgiveness of God. This can only come through faith in Jesus Christ as Saviour and Lord. The crack in the human armour brought about by sin can only be fixed through the shed blood of Jesus Christ. That repair is only guaranteed on the basis of obedience.

The story of Naaman the Syrian Army General who suffered from leprosy gives us another perspective on obedience to the Word of God being the bedrock of recovery (2 Kings 5:1-14). As powerful as Naaman was, he was in desperate need of recovery in his life. The Bible records that Naaman was great and very honourable in the eyes of his master, and that through him, the Lord had given victory to Syria. Whilst his physical condition did not seem to affect his military position, it represented a social stigma. We cannot tell exactly what was going on in Naaman's mind, but from his actions, we can safely conclude that recovery from leprosy was an overriding priority for him.

Naaman had heard through his wife, who had been told by a slave girl from Israel that there was a prophet in Samaria who could heal her master of his leprous condition. Naaman's value to the king of Syria is shown by the fact that the king was willing to write a letter of recommendation on his behalf, wrongly, as it turned out, to the king of Israel.

Naaman's trip did not get off to a very good start. First, he had gone to the king of Israel who complained that the king of Syria was setting him an impossible task, in asking him to heal his key general of his leprosy and that his failure to do so would be used as a pretext to make war against Israel. Fortunately the news filtered through to Elisha the prophet. This encounter was the second hiccup in the general's journey to the land of Israel in search of recovery. When he arrived, Elisha did not even bother to come down from his house to meet him. He simply sent word in the form of an instruction that Naaman should go and dip himself seven times in the river Jordan.

To say that Naaman was not happy with the manner of the consultation he had been given would be an understatement. He was incandescent with rage. Here was a man who could afford the Harley Street doctors of his day, being told by a rag and bone man of a prophet to go and wash in a filthy river in a foreign country. The senior army general turned round and headed home. Were it not for the intervention and wise counsel of one of his servants, Naaman would have missed out on his opportunity for physical recovery. Having calmed down, Naaman went and did what the prophet told him to do, dipping himself in the river Jordan seven times. His leprosy disappeared.

You might be in a situation when it seems that all your efforts and investments have yielded very little or no result. You may have invested financially in commodities or real estate, or sunk your life savings in a business, but instead of breaking even, creditors are on your heels. You may be a pastor who has been labouring so hard, with very little to show for it. You are at your wits end as to what to do. Your situation might even be similar to or worse than that of Peter and his fellow fishermen who had toiled all night but caught nothing (Luke 5:1-11). God has a word for you that is as bold as it is directive: seek His face first, and once you have heard from Him, follow that word. Whatever He says to you, do.

Obedience was the key to what followed in the encounter between Jesus and Peter and his fellow fishermen at the Sea of Galilee. Peter said to Jesus: "Master we have toiled all night, and we caught nothing, but nevertheless at Your word, I will let down the net." The result of that act of obedience was overwhelming - the men caught a large number of fish, so much that their nets began to break. Their haul was so great that they had to call other fishermen to help them manage their catch. God wants to bring recovery in every area of your life, including times of celebration when things sometimes seem to go awry. Obedience is the key.

There is something unusual about Peter's obedience. Nazareth, where Jesus came from was a small village surrounded by hills. Galilee was a major fishing town. As Jesus did not come from a seaside town, He had no right whatsoever telling a seasoned, weather-worn and hard-nosed fisherman what to do. But He did. That is because He has knowledge of all things. He has power over nature and authority over all of His creation. Jesus knows all things and has power to do all things. His word can be relied upon. The fishermen obeyed His words and got a great reward for their simple act of obedience. In the same way, God's power can only become real in your life at the point and place of obedience.

You may be familiar with the story of when Jesus and some of His disciples were at a wedding in Cana, Galilee (John 2:1-11). His mother Mary was there too. At the point when the wedding party was in full swing, they had run out of wine. Mary realised what had happened and informed Jesus about the situation. Why Jesus? Was it His responsibility to provide wine for a wedding? Was He not a guest just like the other people there? How could Mary expect Him to salvage this potentially socially embarrassing situation? Jesus gave His mother a very interesting response: 'Woman, what does your concern have to do with me? My hour has not yet come.'

Mary however was not put off by the awkwardness of the situation and told Jesus' disciples: "Whatever He tells you to do, do."

Even though Jesus had not performed a single miracle prior to that time, His mother knew by revelation that there was something extraordinary about Him. Mary had discovered that the solution at that time resided in one person alone – her son. Jesus later told His disciples to fill six large stone jars with water to the brim. When they had done that, Jesus asked the disciples to take from the filled jars and serve the guests. The disciples did, and averted a major crisis. The chairman of the wedding feast did not have a clue where the wine came from. He thought the celebrant had kept the best wine till the latter part of the party. That recovery from a potentially embarrassing social situation was made possible by the obedience of the disciples to the revelation that Mary had received about Jesus.

Timeless Truths

- Our security lies in what God has said, not what the experts say.

- What is sown in God cannot and will not die.

- Your sacrifice in service to God will be rewarded.

- Obedience to God's Word is the bedrock of total recovery and prosperity.

- God's power can only become real in your life at the point and place of obedience.

Chapter 10

WORK HARD AND SOW
IN THE LAND

Then Isaac sowed in that land, and reaped in the same year a hun-
dredfold; and the Lᴏʀᴅ blessed him. And Isaac dug again the wells
of water which they had dug in the days of Abraham his father, for
the Philistines had stopped them up after the death of Abraham. He
called them by the names which his father had called them. Also
Isaac's servants dug in the valley, and found a well of running
water there. But the herdsmen of Gerar quarrelled with Isaac's
herdsmen, saying, "The water is ours." So he called the name of the
well Esek, because they quarrelled with him. Then they dug another
well, and they quarrelled over that one also. So he called its name
Sitnah. And he moved from there and dug another well, and they
did not quarrel over it. So he called its name Rehoboth, because he
said, "For now the Lᴏʀᴅ has made room for us, and we shall be
fruitful in the land." (Genesis 26: 12, 18-22, NKJV)

THE central lessons in this chapter are set in the context
of a deep awareness that all that we have and are is
by and through the grace of God. There are those who
refer to themselves or are referred to as self-made. Nothing
could be further from the truth. The Bible shows us that we

are who we are by the grace of God. Our hard work is futile without God. The Psalmist recognised this when he said:

Unless the LORD builds the house, the builders labor in vain. Unless the LORD watches over the city, the guards stand watch in vain. (Psalm 127:1)

The book of James says:

Every good and perfect gift is from above, coming down from the Father of the heavenly lights, who does not change like shifting shadows. (James 1:17).

The grace of God not only redeems, it strengthens, enables and empowers the believer to serve, be and become all that God has purposed for him or her. St Paul writes:

For by grace you have been saved through faith, and that not of yourselves; it is the gift of God, not of works, lest anyone should boast. For we are His workmanship, created in Christ Jesus for good works, which God prepared before-hand that we should walk in them.(Ephesians 2:8-10, NKJV)

The grace of God is none other than Jesus Himself at work by His Spirit in the life of a believer.

Again St. Paul wrote:

But by the grace of God I am what I am, and his grace to me was not without effect. No, I worked harder than all of them—yet not I, but the grace of God that was with me. (1 Corinthians 15:10).

And God is able to bless you abundantly, so that in all things at all times, having all that you need, you will abound in every good work. (2 Corinthians 9:8)

Grace, therefore, is God's supernatural enabling or power. It is His ability that He puts in us to function.

So we conclude: it's all by grace. However, you must put yourself in the place of work to work, and then God gives you the grace to be productive and prosperous. That is the mystery of grace and how it works.

We read of Isaac:

'Isaac planted crops in that land and the same year reaped a hundredfold, because the LORD blessed him. The man became rich, and his wealth continued to grow until he became very wealthy. He had so many flocks and herds and servants that the Philistines envied him'
(Genesis 26:12-14).

You need to stay in the land that God has placed and commanded you to remain. Staying in the land is not simply occupying space. The 'land' is the ground from which your blessings, progress and prosperity will come from. This is your local community, your city, your marriage, your family, your work or your business. You may be in recession now or going through a difficult phase, but there is recovery ahead. Your primary assignment or task is to till the ground, sow seed, dig new wells and re-open ancient ones. This task demands the full understanding of what the land, the seed, and the water stands for, particularly as it relates to recovery of any kind, whether spiritual or material.

Sowing the seed of the gospel is a central element of the Church's core mission. It is to make Jesus known through our proclamation and demonstration. The ground is the heart of men, people's lives, families and communities. It's about invading culture – youth and the various sub-cultures in our communities. The work is personal and corporate in nature. Without sowing, there will be no harvest. Isaac sowed in the land that he was staying in and reaped a one hundred-fold harvest. We must do the same – passionately, continuously, tirelessly and expectantly.

God's Word is the seed that we sow. We must re-discover seed-sowing in a big way – using new technology, new communication tools, and new approaches that connect with today's culture. This was one of the hallmarks of the early Church and those who have gone before us. They sowed the seed of the Word of God wherever they went. They started prayer groups and house meetings, and from there local churches grew. That is the New Testament pattern which they followed, with stunning results. Isaac was a seed-carrier and a sower of seeds. We must do the same. The trouble is that we carry seed of the Word, the anointing is within, but we neither sow nor release the unction within.

Not only must we sow, we must also water what we have sown. Water represents a number of things; one of which is the Word of God. It is also a symbol of the Holy Spirit - the life-giving Spirit of God. This is the anointing, which comes through preaching and prayer (as often as possible, with fasting). Faith-filled prayer and action are the means by which the seed is sown and watered. Seed-sowing through the Word is one of the ministry priorities of the Church. The Apostles chose to give themselves to prayer and the preaching of the Word. We must soak the land that we sow in with the Word and that takes hard work. As we play our part, God will do the rest, and the seed will germinate, grow and multiply.

Having spent part of my childhood in a rural setting, where I worked on a farm alongside farmers, I know that farming is a tough and sometimes lonely business. Isaac was a hard worker. He was no idler. He persisted. We must do the same.

Our hard work must be linked to smart work. Just as prosperity brought contention between Lot's herdsmen and those of Abraham (Genesis 13:7ff.), Isaac's prosperity also provoked anger and jealousy from the Philistines. Remember, Isaac was a foreigner in the land. The locals were struggling and starving whilst he was growing and prospering. Abimelech and his people did not recognise that it was God who was blessing Isaac. All they saw was the increasing material wealth of Isaac and his growing power. To them the threat was just too much to ignore. Our world today is no different. Jealousy, criticism and attacks come from many quarters. Like his father before him, Isaac chose to keep the peace. He was smart.

In our contemporary Western world, we have seen recent immigrant communities strive, excel and surpass indigenous and long-established ones. In terms of economic and social mobility, recent incomers are moving ahead of the natives or those that arrived centuries previously. In America, segments of recently-arrived African, Hispanic, and Asian Diaspora, have overtaken their White working class and African-American counterparts in many areas of life. We see similar trends in the United Kingdom, especially in the field of education. Tensions invariably arise, posing major public policy challenges in relation to community cohesion, as inter-communal jealousies and tensions rise.

That aside, hard work has its reward. My late father-in-law

had a mantra for his small family of eight children: 'there is no substitute for hard work.' Isaac worked hard and God blessed him. The first step is one of obedience – sow in the land. Dig new wells and re-dig the ancient ones. A willingness to work hard is the next thing that will position you for the unstoppable flow of God's grace for total recovery and prosperity.

Many people do not need convincing that the recovery from the current economic recession requires hard work. It must be linked to other actions that get to the bottom of what the problems are. The problems we now face are primarily due to the excesses of a world that has been used to living beyond its means for several decades. There is also a need for hard work to convince people that gone are the days when society would continue to tolerate able-bodied men who have fathered 17 children with five women continuing to live on disability benefits while the hard working ones continue to slug it out in offices and factories, just to pay the way for the lazy folks. This requires a major shift in policy, mindset, and ultimately culture. It shouldn't take the hardline approach to persuade society that we can no longer continue to live beyond our means and expect life to be normal. Hard work is also necessary for countries in financial deficit to come out of recession.

Many people will be aware of the story of Japan when the atomic bomb was dropped on Hiroshima and Nagasaki. Japan suffered greatly during and after the Second World War, but as soon as the war ended, Japan began a process of nation rebuilding through hard work and sacrifice. Although the impact of the catastrophic national disaster was felt for a long time in Japan, patriotism, sacrifice and hard work was instrumental to that relatively small nation becoming a major economic force in the world today.

What about difficulties in relationships? Marriage in itself is hard work, and recovery from marital conflict is even harder. There is no two ways about it - if a marriage or any relationship for that matter has to recover, hard work also has to be applied in the same three or four dimensions. Hard work has to be applied first in taking a step back and determining or agreeing that there is a problem. Couples have to be honest enough and humble to seek help. They must seek to find out and discover what their problems are, what God says about the situation and what to do about it.

The command of God is clear in the Bible: "As long as it lies with you, live in peace with all men and women, (paraphrased)." Once you know what God says, you must accept it as final and stop bickering, mudslinging and backbiting. You must work hard to invest in forgiving and forgetting, and allow God to heal the mind of abandonment, abuse, disappointment and hurt. You must again work harder – to discover exactly what God has said about the ingredients of a thriving and successful marital union. Once you discover this, you must apply it. This is called wisdom.

Recovery from a marital situation will not survive on the basis of superficial remorse, empty promises, or blatant attempts to sweep issues under the carpet. Time must be given for sober reflection, re-adjustment, and healing. Change is often a difficult process and individual parties in a difficult relationship must be given time to make changes, but this cannot go on forever. What must first be discovered is the heart of God in your marriage, and upon discovery, you must accept His Word as final. We must then apply what the Word of God dictates irrespective of who has been hurt. Without doing this, the devil would have been given a free rein in families, and recovery will not be achieved.

Organisational and business recovery will also benefit from the same approach as that of individuals and families. Without true discovery, there cannot be a recovery. Companies, corporations, and businesses in a financially dire situation must ask the critical questions about what led them to their current position. You may have wondered why successful businesses spend large amounts of money on consultants, and turn around teams. As much as many people would like to hate these recovery or turnaround specialists for what they are commonly perceived to be, they are the ones usually saddled with the task of getting to the bottom of why a once thriving company now finds itself in a financial mess.

As humans, we don't like to be scrutinized. We find it painful. But to achieve recovery in business, you must look at whether the figures add up, and carefully analyse how you got from A to B, and how to safely get out of the financial conundrum or cul-de-sac. That in itself can be very painful, but without it, recovery may not be fully achieved and the company may well go under.

So for businesses, you must look at the books -whether they have been 'cooked or roasted'; you must check how staff have handled customer services; you must examine how staff have responded to orders and enquiries; you must address interpersonal relationships among staff, whether there has been healthy competition or a destructive one. You must look into how employees have conducted business, how managers have handled their business units, and how the directors have managed human and financial resources and stakeholders. The entire business must re-appraise the structure, the culture and the function with a fine tooth comb. Without that kind of review, sustainable recovery will not materialize.

In the annals of major corporate recovery, the story of Steve Jobs and the Apple Computers stands out as an example par excellence of how to discover in order to recover. Once we know and discover what the problems are, we then have to determine what God says about the situation. The discovery must be followed by what to do - application of the right principles and methods, and then allow time for things to take shape. It requires focus, discipline and hard work. Without them, recovery will not happen.

Timeless Truths

- Sowing the seed of the gospel is a central element of the Church's core mission.

- Seed-sowing through the Word is one of the ministry priorities of the Church.

- A willingness to work hard positions you for unstoppable flow of God's grace for recovery and prosperity.

- Our hard work must be linked to smart work.

Chapter 11

BE WISE AND FLEXIBLE

Then Abimelek said to Isaac, "Move away from us; you have
become too powerful for us." So Isaac moved away from there
and encamped in the Valley of Gerar, where he settled. Isaac's
servants dug in the valley and discovered a well of fresh water
there. But the herders of Gerar quarreled with those of Isaac and
said, "The water is ours!" So he named the well Esek, because they
disputed with him. Then they dug another well, but they quarreled
over that one also; so he named it Sitnah. He moved on from
there and dug another well, and no one quarreled over it. He
named it Rehoboth, saying, "Now the LORD has given us room
and we will flourish in the land."
(Genesis 26: 16-17, 19-22)

W<small>E</small> live in a rapidly changing world. People change.
Seasons change. Circumstances change. Change
is the only constant in life. The constancy of and
necessity for change is the perennial challenge facing everyone, including those in politics. It is beautifully captured in
the words of former British Prime Minister, Harold Macmil-
lan (later ennobled as Lord Stockton). When asked what a

prime minister most feared, he responded in his typically patrician manner: 'Events, dear boy, events.'

What Lord Stockton's pithy response succinctly conveys is the risks attached to sudden changes in the world in which we live. Isaac's world was no exception. He lived in a volatile, hostile and sometimes violent environment. Biblical history clearly shows that this was an age and region where tribal wars and skirmishes between clans was a regular feature of life. So, even though God had told him to stay in the land, and re-affirmed the Abrahamic promises to him, it was not an incident-or-trouble-free package. Accordingly, Isaac needed not only to work hard but smart. **That is because every seemingly dangerous shift, every threat or apparent danger, is but an opportunity in disguise**.

Being flexible requires awareness, sensitivity, and openness to possibilities and options. This includes what you do, how you work, where you work, and who you work with. Without being smart, flexible or creative, you might end up like the dinosaurs. This is true for individuals and communities.

In what ways then can you be flexible and smart as you recover from any situation and in an economic downturn? The Bible indicates that Isaac had been a herdsman. Being a herdsman meant that he could move at short notice with his family. However, we read that he 'sowed in that land'. Sowing in the land shows two things. First, he had added arable farming to animal husbandry. Arable farming is one that is dedicated to grains, while animal husbandry is farming that deals with cattle, sheep, goats and the like. Second, Isaac was prepared to adapt, growing cash crops instead of only rearing animals. Cash crops are plants that are cultivated with the market in mind. The seed is planted, harvested and sold for cash. So Isaac had added another dimension to his farming business; he was handling animals as well as crops.

Isaac's success however bred enemies. Haters and enemies of progress of other people's success emerge, even when it is God who has blessed you. Scientists say that biologically we are wired with only two ways of dealing with our enemies: flight or fight. Isaac seems to choose flight. There are of course times when we must confront evil and things that are simply wrong. That is an important responsibility that we have as individuals. However, Isaac's example teaches us that there are situations when the right thing to do is to simply move on or move away. So, when confronted by aggressive and violent opposition, he moved on without moving out. He moved from Gerar (Genesis 26:6, 16-17). He re-opened the wells previously dug by his father. Isaac moved two more times before settling down at the third attempt (Genesis 26:19-22).

Isaac was flexible in his response to a changing situation. He not only tapped into what was already there (wells and water), he was willing to move when the immediate environment proved hostile; without moving away from the land of promised blessing. He did not move out of the land into Egypt, but moved around the land in search of water. What was important to him was land. If there was land, he would exert himself and dig a well. We must do the same – keep tilling the ground, moving forward until God settles us in our own spacious place. Isaac's strategy was to move if there was conflict. It would seem that conflict was a barometer by which he judged whether it was the will of God for him to permanently pitch his tent in a given location or not. May God grant us wisdom to be more agile, mobile, flexible and hard-working. Amen.

Isaac was flexible in his approach; we must do the same. For some people flexibility and mobility may take the form of retraining, working different schedules, or travelling further afield until the recession is over. I know a lady who worked and lived for a year in a city over one hundred miles from her family home. She came home at weekends, put in place what she could for her husband and young family, before hitting the highway very early each Monday morning. She then got a job closer home. But when that came to an end, she was off again to another distant location. As I write, she travels over 200 miles away from home to work as a consultant on two client sites. She has been flexible in her response to what was a very challenging set of circumstances. In contrast, some people give all kinds of reasons why they cannot travel far, whilst the real reason is their resistance to respond flexibly to change.

Flexibility in matters of recovery does not necessarily mean that you quit or that you play dead. It demands that you deploy the use of new tools, new techniques, new approaches, and build new alliances.

A flexible approach requires that we adapt, adjust and make necessary shifts on the road to total recovery. I will describe below a number of strategies that you can adopt to maintain flexibility on the road to total recovery and prosperity.

Association

You may have heard the saying, 'Show me who your friends are and I will show you who you are.' I remember a number of years ago watching on the television a group of American teenagers who were on a basketball tour in the UK. Every one of those talented boys was from a dangerous housing project in a major city. Each had huge academic potential and excellent sporting ability. Basketball was not merely a diversionary strategy; it was character building for them. When asked why he had joined the basketball club, one of the teenagers gave a response that was telling: 'If you want be the best, you got to hang around with the best.'

Who we run with says much about who we are and where we are heading. Right association helps to keep us alert, disciplined, always learning, growing and making progress.

The most important associate one could have is Jesus. Our intimacy with Him enables us to receive revelation, vision, and direction. Our alliance with Him enables us to see and seize opportunities when they present themselves, and to avoid dangers when they show up. We can enhance our alertness and smart working by connecting with coaches and mentors; people with competence and excellent character, who can provide us with counsel, insight, challenge and support.

Information

As a teenager an uncle gave my brothers and me an edition of the *Guinness Book of Records*. It was one of those 'Wow' gifts. We loved the book and spent hours reading it, being absolutely fascinated by the amazing facts and figures it contained. However, what I recall best is the words the uncle wrote on the inside cover: 'Knowledge is Power'. I will always remember those words. It was an inspiration; a challenge to acquire knowledge. Those words are one of the propellants in my thirst for information and knowledge.

You may have heard it said that we live in an information age. That is no longer true. We now live in what is called the *shift* age, where information changes by the second – on the Internet, on Facebook, on Twitter, and on other media platforms. It was said previously that information in the world doubles every five years, but that is no longer the case. We are now suffering from information overload. The response is not to switch off, but to get smart and get on with it.

Individuals, communities, churches and corporations need to approach the information that is around them in three major ways. The first is to find out which information out there is relevant to you and that will help you towards growth, transformation, and recovery. This is a continuous process. Know your source and be open to new sources. The second is to further filter and analyse the data - looking for insights, trends, and implications. The last step is to ask what it means in terms of your current practice. What do I need to stop doing, or keep doing, or do differently or start doing as a result of the new information that I have to hand? Without asking these crucial questions, we would be bringing the past into the present.

Linked to the discipline of association is the need to keep a look-out for those who could bring transformational insights your way. Information that comes through conversation is one means, but a very important source is books, whether electronic or hard copy. This is an important discipline for leaders or anyone who aspires to being a leader. **Every leader should be a reader**. Reading helps the leader and those who are not in leadership roles to maintain a flexibility of mind, an ability to make connections and apply fresh insights to what they are doing.

Inspiration

Inspiration can come from a variety of sources - from God, from people and their ideas, and from your environment. God inspires us through visions, dreams, prophetic revelations, but primarily through His Word, the Bible. Revelation has been dealt with extensively in the second and third chapters. Isaac must have been given a lift and a renewed zeal to carry on when God spoke to him, instructed him and re-affirmed His promises. We can also draw great inspiration from other people, and I don't mean so we become bland imitators.

I have had the privilege of working with some very talented and highly intelligent people; individuals blessed with the most amazing minds. They had the capacity to see and analyse things with such crystal clarity, and break down complex issues with great ease. It was fascinating to see how their minds worked, how they approached and tackled problems. I loved working with people who helped me raise my game. I learned a great deal from them and drew tremendous inspiration. It is critical that we are honest and humble enough to accept that we are very limited and not good in everything; and so seek to draw inspiration from what others are doing that is good, efficient and effective.

That way one is open to continuous learning and change.

Introspection

The process of remaining flexible, agile, and responsive requires the ability to look within. The previous strategies demand that we look without, whilst introspection calls us to look inside. The dictionary defines introspection as the practice or act *of examining one's own thoughts, impressions, and feelings, especially for long periods*. For recovery to be achieved, introspection cannot be a splash-dash view of events, but a deep search of thoughts and the way things are done; a soul or mind search you might say. 'As a man thinks so his life would come out.' That is so true. The mind is the most versatile machine on the earth. Out of it have come the greatest inventions. Think! Think! Think! Look within the inner recesses of your mind. Bring together all the information, conversations and impressions you have had. Interrogate, analyse, and pray to see what is there but is hidden. Ask God for an 'Ah ha' moment when it seems that a light bulb is being switched on in your mind.

Devotees of everything *Apple* will know that the people who were the architects of Apple Inc., the maker of your *Apple* products – Mac computers, iPods, iPads and the iPhones or Smart phones - were once on the edge of bankruptcy and financial ruin. Today, Apple is the world's second largest information technology company by revenue, after Samsung Electronics, and the world's third largest mobile phone maker after Samsung and Nokia. Apple has been through periods when they made useful but expensive and bulky products that were far from being user friendly.

The company suffered a massive decline between 1986 and 1997 as a consequence. But Apple recovered, through introspection and consumer research. This resulted in the launch of a raft of new cutting-edge products that defined the company in the eyes of the consumer. Without looking inwards, that wouldn't have been possible.

Innovation

Invention is coming up with something that is brand new and which has never been done before. Innovation, on the other hand, is about improving on what already exists - our systems, processes, structures, practices, administration and so on. Invention involves massive or radical leaps, often involving what change management specialists refer to as a discontinuity. In other words, an invention does not just change the rules of the game; it changes the very nature of the game itself.

For example, in the process of industrialisation, communication and travel, the steam engine was a game changer, as was the jet engine when it came. They brought about seismic shifts in the world of work, travel and how people live their lives. For example, the steam engine, the heartbeat of the industrial revolution, transformed the way people worked, large-scale construction, manufacturing and the transportation of goods and people. Similarly, the jet engine radically altered the aviation sector. By contrast innovation is essentially incremental. One sentence to sum up innovation in its entirety is this: 'Anything can get better; things can always improve.'

Collaboration

Collaboration refers to partnership with people of like mind who will help you to get to your goal. Collaboration connotes a bringing together of people and resources. However, partnership does not mean a compromise of one's core values or vision. The principle is well brought out by the story of the prophet's widow in 2 Kings 4:1-7. The widow connected with Elisha the prophet, her neighbours, and her two sons. Partnership is necessitated by the fact that we do not have all the gifts, tools or resources. This applies to individuals, organisations, local churches and denominations. God is challenging us to break out of historical denominational *ghettos* and *prisons* and connect with like-minded *brothers* and *sisters* whose essential purpose and mission is to worship God in Spirit and in truth, and reach the world with the good news of Jesus Christ.

For far too long, pride, fear, petty jealousies and a narrow view of Christ's kingdom has inhibited the Church's mission on earth. The road to total recovery will be marked by increasing collaborations and partnerships. Collaboration calls for a new awareness of the potential for new relationships as they open up in our local, regional and global communities. This would mean partnership between churches, local and central government agencies, charitable organisations, and community groups. In a changing environment, this is absolutely necessary for any kind of recovery.

The secular world and the people of other religions are not the Church's enemies. They should be seen as Christians-to-be. With that perspective and exercising godly wisdom, we can bring them into the kingdom without compromising our beliefs and godly principles.

There is a major lesson to be learned from what happened

in the latter part of Genesis 26. For many years Abimelech the Philistine king and his people had maintained a hostile posture towards Isaac. Eventually he and his people realised that they could not defeat Isaac because God was with him. The blessing of God on Isaac's life was such that they realised there was no point in maintaining a hostile stance. They therefore entered into a classic 'live and let live' treaty with Isaac (Genesis 26:26-31). It meant that Isaac could go forward and keep on prospering, without fear of attack or any form of disturbance. That was an example of accommodation without absorption or assimilation. This shows that collaboration does not necessarily have to be all or nothing. Collaboration without compromise is vital if the Church is to continue on the road to the recovery of lost things.

Infiltration

Culture is moving fast - in all forms of popular music, the arts, and social media. Within what might be defined as core culture there is a multi-layered web of complex sub-cultures. In this confusing mix, the risk that the Church is facing is one of resignation: a mental, emotional, practical, and dare I say it, spiritual checking out. Disconnection and a total inability to grasp what is happening at the grassroots in society; in the youth clubs, streets, in the tough inner city estates around the nation, leads to a justifiable charge of the Church being irrelevant.

This situation is a long way from the biblical ideal which Jesus lived out. He invaded and affected culture. He was and still is the most influential and supremely relevant figure that has ever walked this planet earth. The reason for His relevance is that He met the diverse needs of people – spirit, soul and body. Those who needed physical healing, He healed; those who were hungry, He fed. For the man whose daughter was dead, He raised the girl; the woman with the flow of blood, He healed; the two men who were blind, He gave them sight; the demon possessed mute, He delivered. And those whose lives were adrift and rudderless, He taught the truth while at the same time showing amazing compassion.

Jesus went out and met those on the margins of society. He embraced them and built a relationship with them, through His words and deeds, and brought them into His Father's kingdom. The Church must do the same and invade culture: a world of opportunity made up of individual lives, families, education, government and politics, religion, economy, media, arts, entertainment and sport. The so-called seven mountains must be penetrated with the good news of God's amazing grace. We have hidden in our bunkers long enough. We must not allow our church buildings to become our prisons.

Timeless Truths

- The mind is the most versatile machine on earth.

- The road to total recovery will be marked by increasing collaboration and partnership working.

- Collaboration without compromise is vital if the Church is to continue on the road to the recovery of lost things.

Chapter 12

TAP INTO THE SOURCE OF LIFE

*From there he went up to Beersheba. That night the
LORD appeared to him and said, "I am the God of
your father Abraham. Do not be afraid, for I am with
you; I will bless you and will increase the number of your
descendants for the sake of my servant Abraham." Isaac built an
altar there and called on the name of the LORD. There he pitched
his tent, and there his servants dug a well.*
(Genesis 26:23-25)

I LOVE observing human beings in the workplace, market-place, on the streets, on trains, buses and planes; in small groups, large groups, parties and in church. I have learned as much, if not more, from observation, listening to conversations, being in the midst of great minds, than I have done by simply burying my head in a book. That is not to decry or denigrate the value of books because I love reading. But I have been intrigued by one aspect of human nature. It is that despite the general aversion to change, human beings love the new, the novel, the unusual, and the esoteric. People love that which has not been seen before. There is a buzz and excitement in the air when something new or different appears on the scene. Being humans, Christians are not immune to this tendency.

Just as in the early centuries of her birth, when all sorts of heresies were propounded, the Church today has become a modern day bazaar of tricks, gimmicks and new ideas. However, experience has shown that new does not mean good, better, beneficial, or excellent. Instead of looking for the novel or the esoteric, Isaac simply re-opened the long-blocked wells that his father Abraham had previously dug, as well as digging new ones – looking for the same precious commodity – water – that sustained his father and the generations before.

Water is essential for life and living – for drinking, cooking, washing, and cleaning. In our physical world, anywhere on planet earth, water is a life-giver. Many experts have said that as the process of urbanisation around the world gathers pace, the availability of clean water is going to be critical to human survival. Indeed water is likely to be one of the major triggers of disputes across international borders, and between nations where the resource is scarce. You may also be aware that in their extensive study of the possibility of life outside planet earth, one of the first things space scientists are looking for is water. This is why they would go to great lengths to look for it, celebrating in a major way anytime their space rovers suggest that water once flowed or continues to exist on a planet like Mars.

In ancient cultures, the digging of a well was a statement of intent in two ways: first, it speaks of taking possession of the land and having a permanent residence there; and second, it is a deliberate search or quest for life. Water means life, the absence of it is death. It therefore follows that no digging equals no wells, no water, no life, and certain death. God is calling the Church to dig the old wells and find water. All through the Bible we see that water or rain stands for God's Word and the Spirit of God. It is the Spirit and the Word. Both go together. They are inseparable. The Church of Jesus Christ needs to re-discover the powerful combination and interplay of the Word of God and the Spirit of God.

The fundamental conclusion that we come to is that we need the Word of God and the Spirit of God; the living Word, and the life-giving Spirit; not dead, lifeless, useless doctrines and traditions of men, or practices and ways that have outlived their usefulness. We must (re)discover these ancient wells of life.

In John 6:63, Jesus said:

'The Spirit gives life; the flesh counts for nothing. The words I have spoken to you—they are full of the Spirit and life'

Again we read:

On the last and greatest day of the festival, Jesus stood and said in a loud voice, "Let anyone who is thirsty come to me and drink. Whoever believes in me, as Scripture has said, rivers of living water will flow from within them." By this he meant the Spirit, whom those who believed in him were later to receive. Up to that time the Spirit had not been given, since Jesus had not yet been glorified.
(John 7:37-39)

In another place Jesus prayed for His disciples and those who would believe in Him, referring to the water-like cleansing effect of His Word:

> *'Sanctify them by the truth; your word is truth.*
> *(John 17:17).*

In the book of Revelation we read these words: *He said to me: "It is done. I am the Alpha and the Omega, the Beginning and the End. To the thirsty I will give water without cost from the spring of the water of life. (Revelation 21:6)*

How do we re-discover the ancient wells? The story of the prodigal son in Luke 15:11-32 provides a very good illustration. Although the prodigal son is the central character in this parable, the lessons from his life are universal. Like all of humanity in relation to God, his personal problem or crisis was self-inflicted.

I remember a rather painful episode when a young man made a very bad error of judgment that led to a breakdown of relationship with his colleagues. Some were sympathetic and were looking for a way to bring about reconciliation, which sadly never materialised. During a heated discussion in a meeting held to resolve the issue, an older lady stated rather bluntly, 'He brought it on himself, didn't he?' She was right, he did bring it on himself, but a little bit more grace would have been useful. Before we rush to judge, we are all capable, at odd moments, of wielding the axe of righteous indignation and judgment.

The prodigal son as described in the Bible is a perfect example of someone who had everything going for him – a loving father, a very comfortable home, an enviable lifestyle, and a future inheritance that meant he would live in comfort for the rest of his days. The young man asked his father for his inheritance and took off to a distant land where he had a blast until the money ran out. From that moment onwards everything about his life spiraled downwards.

The prodigal son had three options at that point in his life. First, he could decide to do nothing and stay where he was. Second, he could have said to himself that he had blown it completely, and that there was no way out, and committed suicide. Third, he could have continued what he was doing, eating the scraps meant for the pigs. This third option would have had the consequences of the prodigal son struggling and slowly starving to death. Alternatively, he could have taken to stealing, burglary and robbery. He could have resorted to using guns as a night robber. As a foreigner, he would have been easy to spot, and if caught, he could have been sent to jail for a long period, died there or even be killed. Either way, death would of course have been tragic for him.

Strangely, the prodigal son had hope. He decided not to pursue any of those ghastly options. He chose to do the right thing, which was to embark on a process of recovery. He decided to change his address, from the pigsty to the posh home. This was no easy decision. He had already wasted his inheritance and there was no guarantee he would be taken back by the family he had deserted. For him to go back home, he would have to get through the town centre where every-one would have seen him as a failure. His home, the family home, would have probably been prominent, not the type one could quietly sneak into unnoticed. He would have needed to press the bell, and been accosted first by servants who would probably have asked him who or what he was looking for. But the prodigal son did not allow any of that to bother him; he did the right thing and went back home to his father.

The road to recovery is a tough one, and when you seek to dig into the old wells and tap into the new source of life, as Isaac did, you have to go through the process of recognition, repentance, desire, decision and action.

Recognition

All processes of recovery begin with awareness, which is recognition of the gap between where one is relative to where one should be. The story of the prodigal son amply illustrates this point about recognition. We read: 'when he came to himself…' (Luke 15:17). In other words, as has happened to all of us at some point in our lives, the man came to the place when the light bulb came on in his head. For the first time he came to the place of realisation. He knew there was a huge deficit in his life that needed bridging. It was time to go home. In Isaac's case, famine and death threatened; he realised that the livestock would die and the promises of God over his life would be stalled or delayed if he failed to act. The red alert buttons were on. He knew he had to act and act he did. And if he did not already know the location of the wells his father had dug, he would make enquiries.

Repentance

There cannot be any recovery without genuine repentance; and I am not referring to the "I am sorry I was caught" gesture. The prodigal son made his way back home to his father. The obstacles he faced were huge. Pride, loss of face, humiliation, rejection, and hostility were factors that would have gnawed away in his mind as he contemplated his decision. His crossroads decision was simple: *'to stay in this place and die, or to go back home and beg for forgiveness'*. The prodigal son chose the latter option. His eventual return home, his attitude, and his words paint a very clear picture of what true repentance is. It is a change of mind which is represented by a 180-degree change of direction. Pride, arrogance, self-centredness, and rebellion are replaced by confession, contrition and submission. This is what is required when a person comes to faith in Christ Jesus. We confess and reject our rebellion against God, and submit our life to His rule and reign.

What we see in Isaac is a picture of a man who had totally bought into God's plan for his life. He did not deviate from the blueprint; he simply carried it out to the letter, staying in the land, planting seed, and tapping into the source of life.

Desire

A desire is a longing, a deep and intense hunger for something. It captivates, consumes and drives people to act. It is the prime motivator for action. Human beings are driven by many things; some positive, others negative. Two of the primary drivers of human action are fear and greed; or as some would put it, price or prize. Desire is a projection of our appetite – physical, emotional, psychological or spiritual – towards a person, place or thing. The degree of intensity that you have will determine what actions you are prepared to take.

The best motivator that God wants to see in our heart is love – love for Him and for others. Jesus summarised all the commandments in these words: 'Jesus replied: "'Love the Lord your God with all your heart and with all your soul and with all your mind.' (Matthew 22:37).

The Psalmist captures something of this deep longing after God:

'As the deer pants for streams of water, so my soul pants for you, my God. My soul thirsts for God, for the living God. When can I go and meet with God?
(Psalm 42:1-2)

Repentance and returning to God is not possible without a deep underlying desire. The source of life that created us also offers us forgiveness through His Son Jesus. Desire is a longing to please Him; to fulfil the assignment for which you have been placed here on earth. Isaac was a man on a mission. The revelation he received was the first time that God had spoken to him. It was an instruction and a promise that was personal to him. God had transferred the blessing of his father Abraham to him. Isaac was determined to stay close to the source of life so that the promised blessing might be fulfilled. He was not going to drop the baton as far as the fulfilment of the covenant promises was concerned.

Action

The source and place of life for the prodigal son was at home. He had to go home; back to his father; and back to love that is marked by forgiveness, acceptance, and celebration. His presence at home signified that he was in the place of recovery. He had tapped back into life, literally back from the place of death.

Recovery takes place when we re-dig ancient wells, tapping

into the source of life that is God's Word and His Spirit. These are the keys to revival, renewal, transformation, and preservation. Isaac did that and he prospered. We must do the same – for total recovery in our lives, families, church and communities.

A change of priorities

Prayer and Study

Intimacy with God through prayer and study of the Word are like the numbers one and two. They are next of kin; spiritual siblings, and not distant relatives. These two elements were central to what God did in times past. Prayer helps us to develop intimacy with God. It is a declaration of total dependence on Him. Intimacy with God through reading, study, and meditation of His Word is a vital means of connecting the human spirit with the Holy Spirit. Total recovery is dependent on how willing we are to come as dependent beings, seeking His mind, and listening to His voice for guidance, direction, correction, encouragement, and strength. By so doing we tap into the source of life for total recovery and transformation.

Isaac was a man who knew how to commune with God. As he re-opened the wells which his father Abraham had dug but were filled by the Philistines, he was met with hostility; not once but twice. The first he called 'quarrel', the second, 'enmity'. With each confrontation he moved and opened another one. His re-opening of the third well went unopposed, and he called it the 'spacious place'. Isaac prophesied fruitfulness into his own life. Having moved to Beersheba, he built an altar, called on the name of the Lord, and dug yet another well. His building of an altar and digging of a well were significant for two reasons. First, the altar was his place of communion (prayer) with God. Second, the digging of the well was a direct claim to the land as his. When we pray, we not only commune with God, we invoke the rule and reign of heaven here on earth. When we pray we are effectively declaring: *'Your kingdom come; your will be done on earth, as it is in heaven'* (Matthew 6:10).

Unbeknown to Isaac, **God was using his enemies to drive him towards his destiny.** The Bible says: *'And we know that in all things God works for the good of those who love him, who have been called according to his purpose (Romans 8:28).* Every move that Isaac made in response to the aggression of the Philistines was a step towards greater intimacy and fellowship with God. He also moved further and further into the land of his promise. Once in Beersheba, God appeared and spoke to him: *That night the LORD appeared to him and said, "I am the God of your father Abraham. Do not be afraid, for I am with you; I will bless you and will increase the number of your descendants for the sake of my servant Abraham." (Genesis 26:24).* It is a word of comfort, and the promise of assurance and increase, and Isaac responded in this way: *Isaac built an altar there and called on the name of the LORD. There he pitched his tent, and there his servants dug a well. (Genesis 26:25).*

You must notice the order of Isaac's actions. First, he built an altar, which speaks of intimacy, communion, submission and sacrifice. Second, he prayed at the altar. Third, he pitched his tent and finally, got his servants to dig a well. Isaac re-ordered the priorities of his life. His relationship with God was paramount. He knew that if the presence of God was with him, all would be well and that everything would fall into place. Isaac knew that he was in the centre of God's will, and he tapped into the true source of life. The way Isaac changed the priorities of his life is captured in the words of Jesus: *But seek first His kingdom, and His righteousness; and all these things shall be added to you (Matthew 6:33).*

How then should we live in the midst of a recession or seasons of crises? If we are to become all that God wants us to be, we need revelation; a word from God. We need to listen carefully and hear what God is saying, and make God's Word the basis of our decision-making. We must live obediently to what He has spoken to us. Put another way, we must live by faith. We are called to put God first; and our obedience is an expression of our love for Him. The paying of tithes and offerings, even when things are tight financially is a good example. A few years ago, God led me to tithe out of income that I had already paid tithe on. That was in the middle of another economic downturn but the result was a season of unprecedented financial supply for me and my family.

It is a dangerous thing to try to be like others, to fail to learn from history or to go down to 'Egypt' as Abram did. Like Isaac, you must follow the blueprint: carry the seed of vision and revelation in your heart, obey the Word by staying in the land; sow your life, work hard, pray, and believe God to give you the same hundredfold increase that He gave to Isaac.

There will be times of hostility; times that make you wonder whether God is with you. But He always is! He is merely using these situations to provoke you to use what you already have. You must be agile and mobile in your approach. As God shows you opportunities, you must re-dig ancient wells and dig new ones, using what God has given to you – the seed of His word, the water of the Holy Spirit, and the natural abilities He has endowed you with. When you do this, surely as night follows day, your recovery, transformation, increase, and prosperity will come.

Timeless Truths

- There is a powerful combination and interplay of the Word of God and the Spirit of God.

- All processes of recovery begin with awareness and recognition of the gap between where one is relative to where one should be.

- Unbeknown to Isaac, God was using his enemies to drive him towards his destiny.

- When we pray, we not only commune with God, we invoke the rule and reign of heaven here on earth. When we pray we are effectively declaring: *'Your kingdom come; your will be done on earth, as it is in heaven'*.